TRANSFORM

A 12-WEEK COURSE IN PERSONAL GROWTH & LIFE TRANSFORMATION

by Rachel Eva

**REMOVE YOUR ROADBLOCKS AND CREATE THE LIFE YOU WANT IN ALL AREAS!
OVERCOME PAST LIMITATIONS AND CREATE EFFECTIVE ACTIONS
TO ACHIEVE YOUR GOALS AND LIVE YOUR DREAMS.**

**THIS 12-WEEK COURSE EMPOWERS YOU TO HEAL, CARE AND GROW
ALL FOUR ASPECTS OF THE PHYSICAL, EMOTIONAL, MENTAL AND SPIRITUAL SELF.**

Copyright 2016
Transform
Copyright © 2016 by Rachel Eva
Published by Rachel Eva
Printed in the United States of America
ISBN 978-0-9979344-1-0

All rights reserved. This book or any portion thereof may not be reproduced or used in any manner whatsoever without the express written permission of the publisher except for the use of brief quotations in a book review.

Disclaimer:
All content expressed or implied in this book is provided for information purposes only. The information is not intended to specify a means of diagnosing, treating, curing or preventing cancer or any illness. It is not a substitute for treatment by a qualified medical or healthcare professional who should always be consulted before beginning any health program. Finally, the publisher, author, interviewees, doctors and healthcare practitioners referenced in this book expressly disclaim all responsibility for any liability, loss or risk, personal or otherwise, which is incurred as a consequence, directly or indirectly, of the use, effectiveness, safety or application of any of the procedures, treatments, therapies or recommendations mentioned, herein.

Cover design by: Melody Johnson
Interior book design by: Natalie McGuire Designs
Author's photo by: Jennifer Alyse

Transform • Rachel Eva

Transform • Rachel Eva

CONTENTS

7 - Acknowledgments
9 - Words of Encouragement
10 - About My Journey
15 - Recommendations
17 - Laying A Foundation
27 - Program Overview
29 - Getting Started
32 - Self Discovery Form
95 - Week One: Self Discovery and Wellness Planning
117 - Week Two: Who Are We? What Are Our Stories?
143 - Week Three: Finding Your Truth and Wellness
157 - Week Four: Time and Heart Management
177 - Week Five: Acknowledge Growth and Next Step Challenges
191 - Week Six: Putting Things in Right Order
203 - Week Seven: Self Care
215 - Week Eight: Gratitude and Happiness
227 - Week Nine: Creating Balance
239 - Week Ten: Purpose
249 - Week Eleven: Stepping Into Empowerment and Wellness/Wholeness
263 - Week Twelve: Celebrate!
268 - Next Steps
273 - Recommended Reading & Resources
276 - Notes

Transform • Rachel Eva

ACKNOWLEDGMENTS

Many thanks to all of my teachers over the years who helped me on my path. I'm grateful for the valuable contributions they made to the areas of integrative wellness and holistic health and self development that led to this curriculum. Leaders in integrative and holistic thinking, I salute you!

This book is dedicated to my parents and my daughter. Thank you for being amazing teachers and for sharing my journey. I love you, Lilly, Mom and Dad.

> "Start where you are.
> Use what you have.
> Do what you can."
>
> —Arthur Ashe

WORDS OF ENCOURAGEMENT

No matter what challenges, issues, concerns, fears or frustrations you may be facing regarding your life, I would like to encourage you to trust that you have everything you need to overcome these things WITHIN. You CAN create the life you want. As you read this material, as well as beginning to apply what you learn here, I invite you to trust!

If at any time along your journey you feel frustrated, fearful, negative, self-doubting, insecure or discouraged, I would like to challenge you to apply the following approach or stance: "My story, situation, circumstances and my past do not have to control my future. I have the ability to change my mind and therefore I am empowered to change my life."

ABOUT MY JOURNEY

Why is it important for me to share my journey with you? First, it is important to understand my professional background in order to help you feel trust and safety. There are so many self help books and products out there that you may or may not find helpful. I would like for this book to be helpful to you and for you to understand the foundations of my teachings. Every thing you will learn within this book comes from these places: my professional training and personal experience. I will share tools and information that I used in my professional coaching successfully as well as how I applied these steps to my own personal development. I experienced many difficult things along my journey and I have a passionate commitment to my own healing, growth and transformation. It is important to me that you know that I too have walked a path similar to yours.

MY CAREER

My professional journey in Integrative Health and Wellness began when I was working in the corporate wellness programs department at Bally's in 1994. From there, I stepped into being a life coach and an entrepreneur. Currently I am the founder and head trainer for The Integrative Wellness Academy based in Los Angeles, California.

I created the modality of Integrative Wellness and Life Coaching and the Emotional Clearing Method, which is a technique I developed to help my clients overcome limiting beliefs and negative emotions on both the unconscious and conscious levels. My background and training is as an Integrative Wellness and Life Coach and I am board certified through The Association for Integrative Psychology as a Certified Master Practitioner of Mental and Emotional Release®, a Master Practitioner of Neuro-linguistic Programming (NLP) and a hypnotherapist. In addition, I hold many certifications in the area of health, fitness and wellness modalities, some of which include sports nutrition, personal fitness training, yoga and yoga therapeutics. I have trained in muscle testing and transformational kinesiology, the healing arts of energy work and am a Master Reiki Practitioner.

Over the years I have studied religion, philosophy and psychology extensively. I personally practice spirituality as opposed to being aligned with a particular religion. However, I fully honor any religion or belief that you may have and this program will not conflict with those.

It is my goal to show up to every moment and every situation as both a teacher and a student. Cultivating a state of continual learning is a passion of mine and I spend time studying quantum physics, quantum theory, sociology and ancient healing practices.

I was raised to have an integrative, holistic and scientific perspective. From childhood, I was exposed to and raised with mind-body thinking in terms of health, nutritional healing, plant-based medicine, alternative medicine, meditation and spiritual as well as personal development programs. All of these contributed to the development of a personal integrative wellness practice. As a young child I was introduced to many spiritual and religious practices which have also contributed to my unifying spiritual beliefs.

Over the years as I added to my knowledge base through independent studies, trainings and certification programs and in 2010 opened and operated a Wellness Center where my staff and I served over 900 clients each month in increasing wellness through holistic mind, body and spirit modalities, including Life Coaching. This is where I developed and launched the Integrative Wellness and Life Coach Certification Course. In order to reach more people, I decided to close the Wellness Centers' brick-and-mortar location, begin traveling the world and also offering online courses. Now, I teach individuals personal growth techniques to help them transform their lives in addition to teaching my Integrative Wellness and Life Coaching Certification Course all over the world in person as well as to thousands of students online each year.

MY PERSONAL JOURNEY

Now that my professional credentials are out of the way, I'd like to share more about my life and journey. Having to overcome my own baggage and begin my journey towards health and wellness in mind, body, heart and soul was my real training ground. I invest in the ongoing journey through my thoughts, actions, intention and energy *daily*. I am far from perfect and my path has not always felt good or easy, however it has been a beautiful path because it has been mine.

There are some people who know what they want to do: go to school, follow a specific outlined path and reach their intended target or career goal. This was not the path I took. Mine was unique and self-forged. It came with many bumps and bruises and incredible learnings along the way. I used to ask, "Why couldn't I have learned these lessons while hanging out on the sofa, wrapped in a Snuggie, eating bon-bons and farting rainbows?" Wouldn't it be great if we could get the learnings without any of the negative emotions? Well, that isn't the way life works and just because something doesn't *feel* good, doesn't mean that it isn't good.

I only teach what I have learned, practiced, found effective for myself and what has proven effective for empowering my clients and students. I continue to add to and grow my toolbox of knowledge and resources. The programs I teach are like my own personal journey, ever expanding and changing to add new information as it emerges or as I am ready to learn it.

Also, I am not very concerned with being 'politically correct.' I teach and write like I speak—from my heart—with an intention of love and also with the rough edges of a wacky sailor at times (no, I have never been a sailor and I hope you get the metaphor). Hopefully the stories and metaphors that I share in my teachings will not offend you, and if they do please forgive me.

It is important for me to let you know that I had to overcome a lot of baggage in order to be where I am today and to continue growing. I am still working towards returning to wholeness. It is a process, not an event! I am not going to air my laundry list of issues and damages I had to overcome as a pre-qualifier. That being said it is truly a miracle that I am where I am and committed to continued growth.

THE MENTAL, PHYSICAL, EMOTIONAL & SPIRITUAL ASPECTS OF MY JOURNEY

Mental, emotional, physical and spiritual... these four aspects of self are foundational for every human being. In writing my thoughts about them, may you discover the way they show up in your life.

FIRST: THE SPIRITUAL ASPECTS...

As a young kid I was exposed to many belief systems and practices ranging from the New Age Movement, Buddhism, Hinduism, EST, Transcendental Meditation, Judaism, Christianity, American Indian Traditions, Yoga, Atheism/Agnosticism, psychology and other arts and sciences. I found these all conflicting and very confusing so I pretty much went through an "F-it" phase where I threw my hands up and adopted Frank Sinatra's version of "I Did it My Way" as my personal life theme song. After many years of marching to my own beat, I began diving into each of these belief systems, trying them each on for size, practicing them and eventually I discovered the unifying beliefs and similar teachings as they rose to the top.

My personal beliefs and practices used to come from a place of 'well if this is right, then it means *that other one* is wrong.' I found that type of duality-based thinking to breed no love, unity, growth or harmony in my life, heart or mind so...I let it go. I choose to believe that we each have the right to our own path and that those paths are unique to each individual. My spiritual beliefs are very strong, clear and *inclusive*. There's more than one way to skin a cat, and there are more cats then one. So find your 'cat' and the best way to 'skin it' for you.

The other critical message I want to share here is; there is nothing wrong with your soul (or mine or anyone's for that matter). Each soul is perfect. Souls are not broken or damaged in any way. When we experience spiritual un-health or unbalance it is not a result of a broken or messed up soul. It is a sign that the we need to return to the perfection and wholeness that our souls already have. The soul can only be nurtured back to the harmony or balance of its perfection and wholeness.

SECOND:
THE EMOTIONS & THEIR DYNAMIC ROLES...

As a teen and young adult, my emotions ruled me. If I was angry, my anger was all-encompassing. If I was sad, I could hardly get through the day. I never dealt with (and by that I mean *processed* and then *released*) my emotions in a healthy and effective way. I rolled around in them, magnifying them and then when I couldn't take it anymore, I numbed them and swept them under the rug.

Over the years, I have been through almost every kind of therapy to learn how to become 'happy' or to find peace with my emotions. Through my journeying, I learned to process and release emotions because if they aren't, they get stored in the body and cause physical problems. There are many techniques and philosophies woven into the tapestry of self-care, self-love and techniques for emotional release in this material.

THIRD:
MENTAL, OR THOUGHT LIFE & CONSCIOUS PERCEPTIONS...

For most of my life I had a number of limiting beliefs in place that hindered me from being my truest self; which means understanding, appreciating and fully utilizing my unique gifts and abilities. Many, many years were spent misunderstanding my purpose and practicing the ancient metaphorical art of banging my head against brick walls. I was always a visionary and an outside-the-box thinker, however two beliefs kept me prisoner. The first was that I never knew I was smart. I came from a brilliant father who is an underwater acoustic scientist and mathematician. So, I compared my intellect to my father's. The second thing was that I believed something was wrong with me because I had experienced trauma in my childhood (not from within the family but outside of).

Trauma and feeling un-smart coupled to form the way that I looked at the world. Those two little beliefs were like glasses that colored my view of everything. Once I worked through those limiting beliefs and took off the glasses, it changed my view of myself and the world. I continued researching, studying and doing self-development in the mental area to grow.

FOURTH:
THE PHYSICAL PLANE...

My physical transformation journey was the one I was best known for because I went from an unhealthy, sickly thin smoker with severely herniated discs in my spine and extreme back pain, to a semi-professional athlete. I was able to compete on a national level. Over the years I mastered the art of discipline and completely changed my health. In fact; I went to the far right and became a fitness and nutritional extremist. My routines were highly regimented and created the outward desire while completely sabotaging the harmony and balance I felt in the areas of emotional, mental and spiritual health.

My path—from extremist to balanced wellness in all areas—was a long one. Now I live and act from a place of love, kindness and health. If I want to eat a cookie, I eat the cookie! My nutrition and exercise program is incredibly healthy 80 to 90 percent of the time, but the other times, I allow myself to live a little. "All things in balance" is not just a random motto that I came up with but I used it as a mantra to remind myself *everyday* to find that day's balance moment-by-moment, breath-by-breath. One of my teachers, Ganga White, taught me that "Never is never right; always is always wrong."

I am. I am me. I strive to think, act and resonate my truth from a place of love towards others and myself. Many days I fall short of my goals and choose to move forward again the next day, or with the next breath I inhale. I have come to love the path, love the process and find joy, even amidst the messy painful parts.

You are. You are you. You have chosen this book because you strive to think, act and resonate your truth from a place of love towards yourself and others. There are days when you fall short…and now you will have new techniques to use for choosing to move forward with your next breath, in the moment, hour or within a day's time. You will come to love your path, its process, and all the pain and joy available to you as a human being if you so choose to. I invite you to choose to.

RECOMMENDATIONS

Here are 12 important recommendations for approaching this integrative program that will assist you in your journey to increase wholeness, balance, health, wellness and well-being:

1. Seek.
2. Remain open hearted and open-minded.
3. Be willing to question your ideas, definitions and beliefs and let go of the ones that no longer serve you.
4. Be intentional.
5. Do all that you can, only do your best each day, nothing more and nothing less.
6. Doing at least 10 percent is better than doing zero! All things in balance.
7. Start where you are.
8. Take it one step at a time.
9. Do it with love.
10. Get connected with others who appreciate personal growth and self development.
11. Keep going...*always* keep going.
12. Celebrate every small victory.

This program addresses balance in all four systems that make up *you*: mental, emotional, physical and spiritual. Even though you may be focusing on one specific area at a time, this program invites you towards balance in all areas while also helping you resolve specific problems and achieve specific goals.

The *Transform* program is designed to be done over the span of 12 weeks. This program can be done alone, with a friend or in a group you create. You can choose to do it in fewer weeks or more, depending on how much time, availability and energy you, or the group, has and wants to invest. The program can also be done in continuous loops...start at week one, move through the weekly curriculum all the way through the end of week twelve, then repeat! If you are doing this as a group, at the beginning of each 'loop,' new people can join in. This also gives returning group members an opportunity to work on a new goal or to achieve deeper growth in wellness, transformation and empowerment!

I have had numerous people do the program multiple times and they've told me they get something new out of the program each time. The program continues to "grow you." If your do this as a group and your group chooses to do the program only once, I recommend setting up reunion meetings for the group every few months to check in, recap and dig deeper for continued growth!

But first and foremost, set an intention for your

work with this program by writing it down. Then, *before* you begin (or your group begins meeting), I recommend that you fill out the section on "Getting Started" and read the section on "Goal Setting."

Another recommendation for those creating a group is to actually take one week, the very first one, to meet and get to know each other first before diving into the 12 weeks of weekly curriculum. A great idea is to make the first meeting a potluck meal in order to build community!

LAYING A FOUNDATION

This program is designed to be a resource and a tool for you to overcome the challenges you are currently facing, to break free from the past and the roadblocks you face in order to create the outcomes you desire in the areas of health, relationships, finances, career, family, self-development and spirituality. You may begin using this program with a strong focus on one issue or one area but as you achieve more balance in one area, wellness and wholeness expands to all of the other areas, too.

As one roadblock gets cleared another one in a different area may arise and call for your attention.

WHAT IS HOLISTIC HEALTH & WELLNESS?

The World Health Organization gave the simplest definition of health and wellness: "Health is a state of complete physical, mental and social well-being and not merely the absence of disease or infirmity." This state also applies to all other areas of life in addition to health—relationships, finances, career, family, self-development and spirituality. Wellness is the absence of problems, and it is also life's progression of moving towards the comfort of wholeness and balance in all areas.

WHAT IS HOLISTIC HEALTH?

The Merriam-Webster's dictionary definition of holistic is:
1: of or relating to holism;
2: relating to or concerned with wholes or with complete systems rather than with the analysis of, treatment of, or dissection into parts <*holistic* medicine attempts to treat both the mind and the body> <*holistic* ecology views humans and the environment as a single system>"

In terms of medicine, "holistic" applies to therapies such as naturopathy or chiropractic which have long been considered to be outside the mainstream, allopathic or scientific practices of healing using drugs as treatments.

Holistic refers to the *whole person*—metal, emotional, physical and spiritual! More and more people desire to become holistically well and to be treated as a whole person when in need of health care from an expert or when performing self-care (self-treatment, preventative care practices or any technique or modality a person chooses to proactively address holistic wellness and balance). We need to develop health and self-care for our whole selves in order to be healthy and well.

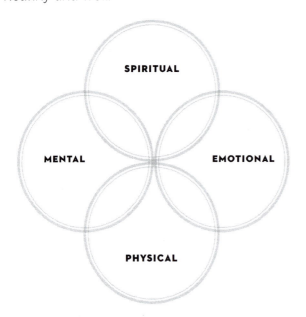

THE FOUR SYSTEMS OF YOU

Holistic or whole person health is health, wholeness and balance in each of the four systems: mental, emotional, physical and spiritual. Since it is easy to have a preconceived notion, label or definition for those words mean, let me break down what I mean by these...

The mental system is your thought life, conscious perceptions, thought patterns, conscious beliefs and models of the world. These are reflected in the way you think, plan, make choices, engage in patterns and it is about how you design your self-image as well as the reality you experience around you.

The emotional system is your emotions, feelings and relationship with and about yourself as well as with others.

The physical system is your physical health and the outer reality you create and experience. This includes the things that you have or do not have on the physical plain around you (finances, organization or lack there of, etc.). The physical system is where the results show up or manifest in your life in a tangible solid way.

The spiritual system is your self-development, your connection to God/Source/Universal Energy/Higher Power (or whatever you define this as), your connection to community, your connection to the world as well as your connection and alignment with your 'true self'.

Holistic health means that there is good health and wholeness in all four systems. Wholeness—and lack of wholeness—is reflected inside the person, outside the body and beyond the body in their environment. Wholeness or balance-and lack of wholeness or balance is also reflected in all four aspects of self; mental, emotional, physical and spiritual as well as effects every major area of life (career, relationships, health, etc.).

The soul is perfect and returning to wholeness brings more balance to the spirit and raises the frequency or the way we experience our spiritual system.

WHAT IS WELLNESS?

The definition of wellness according to the dictionary of Merriam-Webster is: "the quality or state of being in good health especially as an actively sought goal or lifestyles that promote wellness." Do you sense that there is more to this definition? Wellness is different for everyone; it is not a general word to summarize a permanent state of being. Wellness is an ever-moving, ever changing target. Achieving it *as a state of flow, balance and consistency* is both an art and a science.

I describe wellness and health as a state of wholeness and balance in all four systems. Since wellness and balance are more fluid versus fixed states, moving towards wellness is taking intentional actions that lead towards wholeness in the four systems.

What is intentionality? It is your practice of using time, energy, thought, action, habit and choice on purpose! Intentionality is like having a target to aim for. It is saying I intend to achieve. However, setting an intention alone without with the appropriate tools to achieve it alone will not create wellness. Intentional action must be taken. Can you imagine climbing into a row boat on a river without oars or paddles? What would happen? Even if you intended to take that boat all the way to the other side of the river, without putting that intention into effective action by using the tools of paddles or oars what do you think would happen? Exactly! You would drift off to wherever the current of the water took you. In fact, many people live their entire lives this way and approach their wellness this way. Then they wonder 'Why did I crash into the rocky shore? I was trying to get to the other side of this river.'

BALANCE & WELLNESS

Wellness and balance go hand-in-hand. If you have one, then you also have the other. Harmony, wholeness, and balance equals wellness. The word 'balance' can be used as a noun (a thing) or a verb (an action). I think that is a good metaphor for balance itself—it is both a thing and an action! The Merriam-Webster dictionary is useful for defining this good, yet complicated, word: "balance:

1: an instrument for weighing: as
   (a): a beam that is supported freely in the center and has two pans of equal weight suspended from its ends
   (b): a device that uses the elasticity of a spiral spring for measuring weight or force;
2: a means of judging or deciding;
3: a counterbalancing weight, force, or influence;
4: an oscillating wheel operating with a hairspring to regulate the movement of a timepiece;
5: (a): stability produced by even distribution of weight on each side of the vertical axis

(b): equipoise between contrasting, opposing, or interacting elements
(c): equality between the totals of the two sides of an account:
6: (a): an aesthetically pleasing integration of elements
(b): the juxtaposition in writing of syntactically parallel constructions containing similar or contrasting ideas;
7: (a): physical equilibrium
(b): the ability to retain one's balance:
8: (a): weight or force of one side in excess of another
(b): something left over; remainder
(c): an amount in excess especially on the credit side of an account;
9: mental and emotional steadiness.

Noun:
1. An even distribution of weight enabling someone or something to remain upright and steady. 'Slipping in the mud but keeping their balance.'
2. Synonyms: stability, equilibrium, steadiness, footing. 'I tripped and lost my balance.'
3. Stability of one's mind or feelings. 'The way to some kind of peace and personal balance.'
4. A condition in which different elements are equal or in the correct proportions.
5. Harmony of design and proportion.

For every person, every lifestyle and every new twist and turn of life, balance will look very different.

The specific season of a person's life will call for different steps to achieving balance. Finding balance and harmony is a journey of self-discovery and an artful practice of self-love, nurturing and care. No one can tell someone else what balance is or what it looks like during any given stage or season of life—but when you are in a good balance, you know it and enjoy it. When you are out of balance, you know it is time to make changes. Only you can truly know what is or isn't balanced for you and your life!

The physical act of balancing something requires moment-to-moment adjustments. So does achieving holistic wellness; having wholeness and balance within yourself, in your four systems and in each major area of your life. Keeping everything in balance may seem to take a lot of energy—but human life is not the same as walking a tightrope—where focus is a requirement that keeps stress high. Good balance in human life requires paying attention to harmony and rhythm. Even when your life gets a little chaotic—all schedules go through changes and times of busyness and calmness—you can gauge your balance by whether you feel that there is "music" in your life, or a "storm." If you feel the music, you know you are moving in a good direction, even if the beat is fast paced. If you feel the storm, it's time to stop, re-evaluate, make some new decisions and perhaps even take some time out to rest for a bit.

Wellness happens by intention; it doesn't happen by accident. Wellness takes a daily investment of time, energy and intentionality along with intentional actions! Only you can create this for yourself!

WHAT IS WELLNESS & SELF CARE?

Wellness is the care and feeding of the four systems; the mental, emotional, physical and spiritual systems. It is also keeping all things in balance. That is wellness.

Self-care is to take care of your total self in a loving way that leads towards more wholeness in the four systems of self and in each of the major areas of life. Healthy self-care is *always* rooted in love and balance instead of rooted in a need to fix yourself up to be accepted, to be desired, approved or to feel that you are good enough to meet someone else's standards.

There are four very important points or cornerstones to growing in wellness.

1 There is a true and authentic desire to let go of the past, your stories and anything that no longer serves you.

2 The belief that all four aspects of self (mental, emotional, physical and spiritual) are interconnected and the wellness (or lack of wellness) in any one system has an effect on all of the other systems.

3 A willingness to take an honest look at where you are to see what areas of yourself most need balance and growth.

4 Getting and using the right resources and tools, having a plan to measure your accountability, having support and using an effective plan of action.

The *Transform* program will give you a foundation and a framework to build your wellness platform—one on which you can stand and have in place for the rest of your life! This will help you to achieve the goals you set for yourself and to live a happier, healthier and more purpose filled life.

WHAT IS EMPOWERMENT?

The basic definition of empowerment is to give power or authority to authorize someone to take actions or to be a leader.

> *To become empowered means that you are the one who is in charge of the outcomes of living the experiences and feeling the feelings in your own life.*

You are not a victim. You are in charge of your mind and therefore you are in charge of your perceptions, reactions and results.

No matter what you have been through in the past, no matter what challenges you are facing today, you have the ability to become empowered to create the life that you want and experience your desired outcomes. *This does not mean you control the world or make others do as you wish.* It means that you are in charge of how you experience and perceive these things and in charge of the actions you take that will create your life.

RESEARCH ON MIND-BODY-EMOTION-SPIRIT CONNECTION & WELLNESS

In the last 10 years, a lot of research has been done on the mind-body-emotion-spirit connection. The general findings validate truths that have been practiced since ancient times: the interconnectedness of all four systems; mental, emotional, physical and spiritual. I have spent years reading and researching topics related to health, wellness, medical treatments, alternative therapies and the psychological aspects of physical and emotional health. With the help of Google, I suggest that you embark on your own journey of research. It is satisfying to be able to ask your own questions (some examples: "How does emotional, environmental and even unconscious stressors effect the body" and "How does a meditation practice lower blood pressure?").

The basic theory is that all four systems (mental, emotional, physical and spiritual) make up each one of us, are interconnected and impact or affect one another. Health and wellness in one system will affect the others, just as lack of wellness in one area will affect the others.

Throughout human history, there have been many civilizations and cultures that have practiced healing through the principles of holistic interconnection and treatment mentally, emotionally, physically and spiritually. Here is a list of a few:

ANCIENT GREEKS. Ancient Greek medicine was a mixture of theories that were constantly expanding through new ideas and experiments or application, yet the focus was to treat the entire person. Specifically, the ancient Greeks studied the humors, gender, geographic location, social class, diet, trauma, beliefs, and mind set or attitude.

NATIVE AMERICANS. Beliefs, health and the medical practices of Native American people were based on man being part of nature, and health was a question of how balanced a person felt. These people appreciated the world of unseen things and relied on intuition. The deep connection to their intuition was considered a higher form of intelligence then the brain as well as the interpreter of balance in all four aspects of self.

AYURVEDA. A traditional Hindu medicine native to India that focuses on and emphasizes balance. Ayurveda names three elements, the *doshas*, called *vata (water), pitta (fire)* and *kapha (gas or air)*. Balance of these three *doshas* result in health and wholeness in the physical body; imbalance results in illness and or disease.

JUNGIAN PSYCHOLOGY. Carl Jung, a Swiss psychiatrist, psychotherapist and psychologist, developed theories on the connection between spirit and body and how to integrate them. His work was groundbreaking because he identified the conscious mind, unconscious mind, collective unconscious and higher self/consciousness which are very similar to the mental, emotional and spiritual systems I have outlined.

MIND-BODY MEDICINE OR HOLISTIC MEDICINE. This concept and application through new modalities began emerging in the United States during the 1970s. It was introduced as a mind-body connection to healing that included the mental and emotional systems in addition to the physical body. Later the spiritual system began to be included in these as well.

QUANTUM PHYSICS. New developments in quantum physics are reshaping human understanding of nearly everything. If everything is a mass that holds and generates vibration frequency, then things like emotions, thoughts and words have mass and vibrational frequency—energy. Therefore, quantum physics principles relate to health, medicine, energy and spirituality. Quantum theories, when applied to medicine and health, will revolutionize the health care system and make it better. Quantum mechanics is greatly impacting diagnostic tools and technical approaches to treatments.

> *The future of health and wellness rests in the integration of the mental, emotional, physical and spiritual systems.*

Those of you who are reading this are at the forefront of where health, wellness, self-development and medical models are going. Many teachers, counselors, coaches (in all niches) and even leaders in business and politics are recognizing the interconnectedness of all four of the body systems and are adjusting the ways in which they do their jobs. I truly believe that all future healing modalities will be built on the foundation of wholeness and balance in all four systems; mental, emotional, physical and spiritual.

WHAT IS WELLNESS IN ALL FOUR OF YOUR SYSTEMS?

There are so many labels, diagnosis and spoken as well as unspoken expectations flying around in our culture. Some may be helpful, many, if not most of them are not. Why do we have so many labels? Our brains are like a hyper-active personal assistant. The brain grabs tiny bits of information that float by and rush to file it in a way that makes sense based on beliefs and models of the world. We learn these definitions and labels from elders, community or popular culture and they help our personal hyper-active assistant decide where and how to file information as well as how to label and file ourselves, our experiences and thus shaping our reality or at least the experience of it.

Whatever labels and definitions you may have heard about what wholeness, balance, harmony and wellness in all four systems may look like, I invite you to put them on a shelf for a moment and consider this...

Since wellness is fluid versus fixed and it changes moment to moment, day to day, could it be possible that overall wellness in all four systems could be as simple as continuing to take intentional steps, moment by moment, day by day that lead each of the four systems towards more wholeness?

When we experience wholeness in all four systems we also are able to create the things we want to create; experience life with the thoughts and feelings that serve and create peace, love and joy for the greater good of all... we feel and act from a place of congruency or alignment with our true and higher selves all while being... Being connected to a greater power, to all people, to our true selves and the world.

If I were to tell you what YOUR exact experience or feeling of all four systems being in balance would look like, I would only be sharing my label with you. You must discover your own truth in this matter. Just remember that truth will shift as your life shifts.

WHAT IS WELLNESS IN THE MENTAL SYSTEM?

The mental system is the area of your thought life, self-image, perceptions and thought patterns. Wellness in the mental system is a sense of harmony in your thoughts, thought life and thought patterns. This does not mean that you do not experience negative thoughts, those are a part of being human. Also, mental wholeness and wellness provides space, time and allowance for your negative thoughts!

Wellness in the thought life does mean that we are able to manage our thoughts and not end up on a metaphorical hamster wheel running round and round with them. It also means that we are able to experience peace within our thoughts even when we have a strong reaction or preference towards something. It means that we have a happy healthy relationship with our thought life and they do not cause us negative feelings about ourselves and others repeatedly. When we have wellness in our mental system it also means that as beliefs about yourself, others and the world arise we are able to exercise conscious choice in deciding whether those are true or still true for us and if not we are able to let them go in lieu of another belief that serves our greater good.

WHAT IS WELLNESS IN THE AREA OF THE EMOTIONAL SYSTEM?

The emotional system encompasses the emotions and relationship towards and with ourself and others. When wellness and wholeness in the emotional system is present, it looks and feels like freedom from negative emotions of the past; the ability to love and receive love; the ability to process and release emotions in a healthy way; having rapport with the unconscious mind; and, acting from a place of congruency or being true to yourself.

Your status of emotional wholeness does not mean that other people will act in ways you need or want them to; it does mean that you will 'show up' in healthier ways in relationships, choose to build better relationships and attract people who are more whole into your life. It also means that no matter what happens within your relationships, they will not control your wellbeing emotionally, nor will they control your balance and wellness.

Negative emotions are also a part of being human and creating balance and wholeness in the emotional system honors and recognizes negative emotions. Emotional wellness and wholeness means that you'll be able to process and release negative emotions instead of storing them in any of your four systems.

It is critical to reframe the experience of negative emotions to: Just because something feels bad or negative doesn't mean it is completely bad or negative. As a human, you are wired with an ability to feel positive and negative emotions for a reason. Fear is an alarm, within the parasympathetic & sympathetic nervous systems or the 'fight or flight' response, and is designed (when used appropriate ways) to keep you safe. Anxiety is one of the body's warnings that there is something you need to pay attention to. Anxiety can also arise when you have been ignoring your gut instincts or intuition. You can't remove your humanness! It is natural to want to avoid emotions that don't feel good, however avoiding them, suppressing them or sweeping them under the table doesn't make them go away. The feelings are feedback. Instead, choose to embrace them and learn from them. Listen to yourself (your gut or intuition), get the learnings, process emotions in healthy ways and then release them when it is time to do so.

WHAT IS WELLNESS IN THE PHYSICAL SYSTEM?

The physical system is where the 'results' of balance or lack of balance in all other areas, including the physical show up. It is our physical health and it is also all of the physical things we experience around us. These are the tangible things we have or do not have such as chaos, a house or car, clutter, financial well-being or debt.

Wellness in the physical system in regards to health is not just the absence of illness and disease. Have you seen how many of your traditional medical doctors who practice Western medicine view health as the presence or absence of disease symptoms?

The focus on prevention in health has been a step towards wholeness and wellness in the physical system regarding health within the western culture. People are now much clearer about the interconnection of all four of the systems. And, as people move towards balance in the physical system they must take the other three: mental, emotional and spiritual into consideration. What moves towards balance on the physical system must also lead towards more wholeness and harmony within the other systems.

Here's an example: A person who achieves 'ripped abs' at the cost of honoring their work responsibilities is not a win and can lead towards more imbalances (and even to the extreme, getting fired). Having sculpted abs was not a step towards wholeness if it was not achieved through a balanced strategy or steps to get them and effort also spent in the other systems.

So we can say that wellness in the physical system is the continual healthy state of a person who is moving towards even more health, strength, energy, success, ability and stability in their physical body and physical world. Again, this includes all the things that a person has or creates physically around them; for example: home, organization, car, finances or financial health, etc.

WHAT IS WELLNESS IN THE SPIRITUAL SYSTEM?

Wellness or wholeness in the spiritual is simply to return to the perfect wholeness that is. In the spiritual system, wellness is defined as a connection to God, higher consciousness, source, Divine, higher power, energy or whatever your personal definition may be as well as a connection to your true self or higher self, the ability to act from a place of alignments with your true self, and the connection to all people (community) and the world. You may have your own unique definition of this concept—if it works for you, then all is well. It may help to find someone to discuss these ideas with you.

The state of wholeness is a balanced and intentional connection that moves you towards wellness in other areas of your life, your relationships, the work you do, the enjoyment you derive from play, your attitudes and beliefs. This connection can be practiced and expanded or grown in a number of different ways. The best ways for you will be the ones that you feel aligned with. Spiritual wellness is more than a specific religion, spiritual practice or belief system and there are many actions that you can take to move the entire spiritual system to greater wellness or the return to wholeness.

SPIRITUAL WELLNESS VERSUS RELIGION

Religion or any specific spiritual practice is an option one may choose to express, connect and grow. It is not the spiritual system itself, it is an example of an action that can be taken to increase balance within the spiritual system. If you choose to practice within the boundaries of a certain religion, be sure that it is in alignment with your own beliefs. Practicing a religion is not necessary for spiritual growth and balance in the spiritual system.

For some people, joining a community of like-minded/hearted people represents the idea of religious practice. Any organization or group that offers consistency, a sense of calmness and happiness, an appropriate place for the practice of worship, meditation, prayer, contemplation, gentle guidance rooted in love and acceptance, and good support of its members may be of value to you in your spiritual journey. Some people may find this kind of community at a yoga studio, in a meditation group, in a study group or in a support group. Another example of connection for growth in the spiritual system besides religious churches or temples is building/joining a community. A community of like-minded people who are seeking and investing energy in growth in this area can be another choice you can make if this FEELS congruent to you (something that feels true to who you are and what you believe).

DEFINING THE HIGHER POWER OR "GOD"

Respect and honor your belief, intuition and definition of God, a higher power, higher consciousness, divine, source or energy. If you do not have a definition, belief or personal understanding of a higher power or God, or if you have one that is attached to negative experiences, I recommend investigating broader definitions and options in order to find a positive one—one that is rooted in love—that you can choose to agree with and practice. Even if that is simply a practice of LOVE.

Your definition of this can be *anything* that feels true for you. Sometimes, for people who have had negative experiences in religious settings (especially in their youth), they 'threw out the baby with the bath water' and chose to separate from God when they separated from the religious practice. In these cases, or cases of people who have never had belief in God or anything else, the concepts of quantum physics (science), energy and even the phrase "God is love" can be beneficial in creating and developing a new belief that serves their personal, spiritual growth.

PROGRAM OVERVIEW

Each week over the course of this program, your time will be spent in:

- Intentional actions towards balance, wellness and wholeness
- Focused steps towards growth in all four of your systems: mental, emotional, physical and spiritual
- The overall wellness program, with various topics to study and assignments
- Self accountability and connection

If you are doing this program as a group, each week the group should stick to a 60 to 90-minute meeting. When sharing within the group, please limit the time for each person sharing personal stories to two to four minutes per person (depending how big your group is).

It is critically important that everyone has the ability to contribute to the conversations.

People who have extroverted personalities should give those who are introverted a safe space to participate by waiting to share, or by drawing others into the discussion. Group leaders/facilitators should encourage the quieter participants to share but also to respect any person's desire to refrain from speaking. Everyone learns from each other's journeys and stories; each person has valuable things to contribute to the program!

This program runs for 12 weeks. I recommend having an introductory group meeting at the very beginning—before the 12 weeks of weekly materials get covered. That very first meeting is a time to connect, get to know one another, get introduced to the materials and structure of the program, and to identify areas to work on. The last meeting is meant to be a celebration and can include a field trip and/or graduation ceremony if the group desires!

The group members will work on assignments on their own or with an accountability partner. Again, there is no need to be in a group for this program to work for you, I have seen powerful results for those working on this by themselves! I only offer the group instructions for those who want to create a community support around this program.

There will be weekly assignments as well as three assignments that will be worked on throughout the program and completed by the end of the 12 weeks.

THE THREE 12-WEEK LONG ASSIGNMENTS ARE:

1. Create your personal Wellness Action Plan.
2. Take daily action steps in your Wellness Action Plan.
3. Write in a Daily Wellness Journal.

Do what you can and only that—avoid feeling overwhelmed by the work. If you only have five minutes a day to invest in this program, it will still help you. You can choose to do a little or you can choose to do it all. This is your journey! Let me say it again: *do not allow this program to make you feel overwhelmed!* Do whatever you can do. One former participant said that he looked at his schedule and decided that he could "carve 15 minutes out of the day" for *anything* that would lead to self improvement.

This book and program experience will be yours to continue working on forever. You can always come back and do more or repeat a section. This is your journey and this curriculum will serve you beyond the time and space of the programs 12-week cycle.

Give it your best, and know that your best may look different week to week. One week you may be able to do all the assignments, the next you may not. Remember, *this is your journey and… all things in balance!*

GETTING STARTED

If you are working in a group, the group will be your support system, sounding board and accountability in your process. If you are working on your own find ways to lovingly hold yourself accountable as well as to get support from your loved ones during the process.

Always check with your doctor before starting or changing any wellness, exercise or nutritional program to make sure it is right for you. Also, if you are or do experience emotional issues, depression or thoughts of self-harm *immediately* reach out to a professional for help!

Fill out the Self Discovery Form (included in section entitled 'Getting Started') prior to beginning the first week's materials. It is always good to have a little time to marinate on your answers before starting your experience of this program. Here is what to expect in your weeks ahead as you journey through this material:

WEEK ONE: Self Discovery and Wellness Planning
WEEK TWO: Who Are We? What Are Our Stories?
WEEK THREE: Finding Your Truth and Wellness
WEEK FOUR: Time and Heart Management
WEEK FIVE: Acknowledge Growth & Next Step Challenges
WEEK SIX: Putting Things in Right Order
WEEK SEVEN: Self Care
WEEK EIGHT: Gratitude and Happiness
WEEK NINE: Creating Balance
WEEK TEN: Purpose
WEEK ELEVEN: Stepping Into Empowerment & Wellness/Wholeness
WEEK TWELVE: Celebrate!
NEXT STEPS

Now, why are you here?

Why are you reading this book and doing this program? It is important to get *intentional* as you move forward. At the same time it's important to have understanding and clarity about the 'what's and why's' of your past *unintentional* patterns of your life, self-care and treatment. Getting honest with yourself is the most important place to begin your journey to *Transform*.

Read the following testimonial statements of others who've experienced this program and their recommendations for using it:

"I knew that self-care was one of my biggest weaknesses in life. I needed to learn how to take care of myself in a way that honored myself. For anyone getting ready to take this program, I would say: just show up! It's half the battle, and don't be too hard on yourself. Have fun! The results will come if you do the work. It's not about the end goal, it's about the journey."
~ Jessika

"I had just gotten out of a four-year relationship and I was going through an emotional roller-coaster. I had gained 26 pounds then lost 30 pounds due to severe anxiety, and then gained 26 pounds again due to eating and drinking excessively. I was so out of balance in my life. I knew I just needed balance in my life and that my life was unmanageable. I took this program for wisdom. I advise others to be committed, not give up, and be consistent."
~ Reyna

"Make a commitment to stick with it!"
~ Maddy

"I knew it was what I needed in my next season, a health transformation, full body, mind, emotion and spirit approach. I wanted to find a whole life approach to make a change not just one piece of it, which neglects the 'why.' I found tremendous benefit from the 'whole' person approach; not focusing on just our food or just our body or just our mind, but seeing how they all work together for or against us. Commit to every week, expect healing to take place, accept and enjoy it when it does."
~ Gabrielle

THE SELF DISCOVERY FORM

Now it's your turn. Please fill out as much of the Self Discovery Form as possible. The purpose of your Self Discovery Form is to help you learn more about yourself, your roadblocks, beliefs, and patterns that work and do not work in your life. The Self Discovery Form is a starting point from which to achieve your goals. Putting the answers down on paper gives you clarity and accountability. The more open and honest you are with yourself, the stronger your experience and success will be. Once you have answered these questions you'll use these answers to create your personal Wellness Action Plan by filling out the graph exercise, so please keep your answers handy.

Some people do this form all at one time and others find it more helpful to take it a few questions at a time. If you spread out completing this form make sure to marinate on the questions and see what comes up for you. If you choose to sit down and fill it out all at once I recommend setting it aside for a few days while you reflect on it and then come back and review your answers, adding anything that may have come up.

SELF DISCOVERY FORM

Name: Jennifer

Age: 47

Date: May 13, 2020

Accountability Partner's Name (pick someone who can be a loving support for you during this program that you can connect with and talk to):

What are the reasons (problems, challenges, circumstances) that you are doing this program?

Looking to feel more balanced.

The problems I most need to change or resolve in my life are (this can also be something you want to achieve such as a goal):

I want to consider to continue to work on physical health — I want to develop my confidence, connect more spiritually & work on being more intuitive. I want to develop better habits for wellness over all

On a scale of 1 to 10 (1 = least; 10 = most) how intensely do you experience this problem (or need to achieve your goal)?

1 2 3 4 5 6 7 8 **(9)** 10

List what you have done so far to try to resolve the problem or what steps have you taken to achieve your goal?

I've been doing tons of self coaching - reading, quit drinking w/ a program that helped manage thoughts. Attend weekly ww meetings. Try to journal, occasional meditation - therapy, gratitude journal.

List why or how these problems affect your life:

I sometimes feel super disconnected & that leads to depression. I tend to want to numb my emotions & feelings & that leads to bad habits like drinking or eating. Because I hate confrontation I often bury feelings or ignore my gut which leads also back to feeling bad - ignored, insignificant, unheard - which I buffer w/ those same bad habits.

How long has this been a problem, desire to change or struggle in your life?

My whole life this has shown up as an issue

When was it not a problem or a need in your life?

As a personal assistant, burying voice & going along w/ flow is a benefit. When I was deep in denial about what I really wanted it didn't seem to be a need to address

What specifically created this problem or need? What steps led up to it?

Being "shut down" by a very loud + dominating dad + wanting to "keep peace". Learning to go w/ flow, + avoid confrontation served to keep things feel calm + less chaotic. But that shutting down led to me sacrificing my voice, my gut + my sense of self-worth. I adopted other's opinions, didn't trust my own. I self soothed to cover pain of giving up my identity, it made me insecure.

How do you feel about the problem or the need (what emotions are present)?

I feel excited to work on it more. I feel afraid to start "being me" more. I feel sad, confused, regretful that I lived so much of my life w/ my voice stifled. I feel grateful for life lessons + new perspective.

Write about your family and childhood as it relates to the problem or issue.

As mentioned Dad shut us down - He could be bully-like - Loud when his needs/way wasn't met. Easily angered. Mom mostly "appeased" + didn't like to rock boat. Dad had volatile relationship w/ Aunt + Grandma + they were important people to me. Often felt in the middle. Torn + like I couldn't take sides or felt like I was betraying family. Wanted to be "good" kid w/ good grades. Wanted to people please. - Never felt good enough.

Is there a purpose or a reason for having this problem or issue?

Yes. "Peace", happiness, not having to deal w/ confrontation, feeling a sense of security in people loving me. I was insecure in appearance + stuff - As long as I was nice, easy-going, bunny - there was something likable about me.

How will you know when the problem has totally disappeared or when the goal has been accomplished (what will that look like or feel like)?

I will feel comfortable w/ expressing my needs & feelings. I will accept being uncomfortable in confrontation before swallowing my voice. I won't need to numb emotions b/c I will be able to work thru them. I will be better in tune w/ my gut & intuition. I can have tough conversations + come out w/ head high.

How will it feel and what will it look like in your life when the problem is gone or when the issue is resolved?

I will be strong, proud, empowered & respected. I will be at peace w/ my thoughts & decisions. I will not be trying to hide, deny or numb my voice, intuition or values. I will be living balanced.

Are you willing to take the steps necessary in order to release the problem from your life and to resolve the problem, achieve the goal or experience what you do want to experience?

Yes.

On a scale of 1 to 10 how committed are you willing to be with your time, energy and resources towards overcoming this problem or resolving the issue?

1 2 3 4 5 6 7 (8) 9 10

My biggest goals are:

1. Reach healthy weight & physical body / nutrition
2. Feel more connected w/ family, friends / self
3. Become successful life coach & mentor (Podcaster)
4. Manifest lifestyle desired
5. Utilize time better

The areas I struggle most in are:

1. Time management
2. Prioritizing tasks
3. Not buffering w/ social media & other distractions
4. Confidence / second guessing myself
5. Pushing to do tasks "I don't like" or am not good at like meditation & yoga
6. Being consistent on things like + exercise / journal
7. "Speaking up"
8. Overcoming & recognizing neg. thoughts

I spend most of my time on or doing:

I spend a lot of time on thinking about:

My definition of success in life is:

My definition of happiness is:

My definition of health is:

What area of your life would you most like to improve: health, relationships, family, finances, career, spirituality, self-development or something else unique to you?

What areas are your main areas of struggle or that are the most challenging for you: family, relationships, career, finances, health, spirituality, self-awareness, self-development or something else unique to you?

Do you struggle to find balance between your fitness needs, personal needs, life tasks, social life and work? If yes, when time, energy or money is tight which is the first area you cut down on?

What do you find most challenging in life (relationships, work, money, family, etc.)?

What is more challenging for you: balance or discipline?

What areas would you like to see healing, changes or growth in?

What are some of the things that you feel limit you in growth, keep you from achieving your goals or block you from living to your fullest ability?

What are you most passionate about in life?

Do you feel that you are living your purpose?

What would you like to feel or be different, better or more in your life?

What would you like to have, be or do more of in your life?

What do you think are the most beautiful, positive things about the world?

What do you think are the worst things in the world?

What are you most grateful for in your life?

When you have had a long day and really need to 'recharge' would you choose to be home and have some alone time or go out and socially interact?

When you experience stress, negative feelings and or emotions what do you typically do to deal with them?

What do you do to avoid feeling uncomfortable? Please list both positive and negative ways (helpful and not helpful) you deal with this feeling.

How do you escape or process your unwanted feelings? Please list both positive and negative (helpful and not helpful) ways you deal with them.

Write down your average daily food intake (meals and what they are made up of as well as what time of the day you eat them):

What do you feel are your biggest challenges with diet and nutrition?

What stores or markets do you purchase groceries from?

How often do you eat dairy products?

How often do you eat grains or wheat products (rice, quinoa, oatmeal, bread, pasta, etc.)?

What is your guilty pleasure in food or drink?

What favorite foods and drinks can you not live without?

What foods do you really like?

What foods do you really dislike or have a negative reaction to?

What is your favorite meal?

What time of day or night do you crave your favorite things?

How often do you eat potato chips, corn chips or similar salted snack foods?

How often, how much and what kind of alcohol do you consume?

How many servings or fruit do you eat every day?

How many servings of vegetables do you eat every day?

What sources of and how much protein do you eat every day (fish, chicken, eggs, meat, protein powder, etc.)?

How many servings of grains (rice, bread, oatmeal, quinoa, barley) do you eat per day and what kind?

How much water (how many 8 oz. glasses) do you consume per day?

Which describes what your typical eating habit is: stop eating when you feel full; stop eating when your plate is empty; go back for a second helping; forget to eat or something unique to you?

Do you eat quickly, at a normal speed or slowly?

How many times per day do you eat?

How many sweets (candy, sugar, deserts) do you eat per day or per week?

How many of your daily meals have condiments or dressings on them?

How often do you eat canned, pre-prepared or frozen foods? What kinds?

How many times per week do you eat pre-prepared meals (packaged) at restaurants, cafés or fast food suppliers?

How many caffeinated beverages (coffee, tea, soda) do you drink per day or per week and what kind?

What do you feel are your biggest challenges with exercise?

How often do you exercise and for how long each session?

How long have you been exercising and are you consistent?

Did you or do you play any sports? Did you play sports in high school or college?

What physical activities do you most enjoy (dancing, biking, hiking, surfing, etc.)?

What hobbies do you enjoy in life or what things do like to do/want to do for fun (can be physical or non-physical)?

What do you least enjoy about exercise?

What areas of your body do you feel are your strongest?

What areas of your body do you feel are your weakest?

What areas of or aspects of your physical body or physical health do you want to see the most change in?

Would you characterize your cardiovascular ability as good, average or poor?

Would you characterize your flexibility as good, average or poor?

Do you start exercise programs and find it is hard to stick to them or to continue them after a period of time?

What is the biggest reason, challenge or goal in your physical health or physical life (the things around you such as your financial health) that you want to work on in this program?

What is your biggest or most important goal to achieve in your fitness and health?

What would you like to be different, better or more in your physical world (health, fitness, nutrition, and/or the things you own that create your outer environment)?

Please write a brief medical, personal and family history. Please include dates next to any illness, injury, major life change or loss. Please make sure to list any medical conditions and medications (include dosage):

Medical:

Personal:

Family:

What is your genetic as well as cultural background (please list both sides of the family and their approximate year of birth. Example: African American (father), Middle Eastern (mother), culturally raised in Middle Eastern environment (food, traditions, etc.), grew up in Nebraska).

Please describe your current state of health in your physical body:

Do you smoke cigarettes or use drugs, if so how many/much and how often?

Do you have high blood pressure or high cholesterol?

When did you last have blood work done? What were your results?

Date of last physical?

Date of last eye exam?

Date of last dental exam/cleaning?

Are you overweight or underweight? If so, by how much?

Is there a history of mental illness or depression for you or anyone in your family, including those you live with?

Any family members with mental illness, depression, heart disease, diabetes, cancer, obesity, eating disorders, other diseases, illnesses or conditions?

Do you take vitamins and/or supplements, and if so, what kind and how often?

Are you on any medications? Please list dosage and information in detail again here.

Have you been diagnosed with any illnesses, diseases or disorders? Have you experienced a cure or healing from any diagnosed disorder or disease?

Have you ever received any advice or warnings regarding physical exercise by a doctor? If so, what?

How many days and hours per week do you work?

Do you enjoy your job? If yes, what specifically about it do you enjoy? If no, what specifically about it do you find unsatisfying? Do you feel that you are doing what you are created to do? Are you 'living your dream?'

How many hours per night do you sleep?

How often do you go on vacation? When was your last vacation, where was it and how long were you there?

What was your favorite vacation and why?

How much time do you spend outdoors? When outdoors, what activities do you do (walking the dog, gardening, going to the beach, outdoor cafés, etc.)?

What would you like to be different, better or more in your emotional life (feelings, emotions, relationships—with self and others)?

Would you consider your upbringing healthy or dysfunctional and why?

Who do you spend most of your time with? Is that relationship satisfying?

What is your social activity level in your community? Do you have a group of friends you see regularly?

Have you experienced physical, emotional, verbal, spiritual or sexual abuse?

What recreational (enjoyable and relaxing) things do you enjoy? How often do you do them?

What do you like about yourself? What don't you like about yourself?

Do you have negative emotions that you still feel now that have to do with things that have happened in the past?

Do you have any anger, resentments or un-forgiveness towards any person, place, thing or situation (including God)?

How often to you see or speak to friends?

Write a brief description of how you have perceived yourself (your mind, body, etc.) for the majority of your life and any recent changes to that?

Write a brief description of your relationship to food, exercise and self-care in the past and present:

Write a brief description of your relationship with yourself in the past and present?

Write a brief description of your relationships with others (family, friends, and lovers/partners) in the past and present:

Do you feel very satisfied, moderately satisfied or dissatisfied with your life most of the time?

Are you single or in a relationship? If you are single are married or in a relationship, how often do you and your partner go on dates with each other?

Are you happy with your relationship and/or relationship status? Is it fulfilling? What could make it more fulfilling?

Are you satisfied with your sex life? Is there anything specific that you would like to be better, different or more?

When something upsets you, do you tend to get angry, get sad, get frustrated, shut down, scream, cry, ignore it or talk about it, etc.?

What have been the most significant losses and major life changes that you have experienced?

When you experienced these losses/changes, what coping tools did you use to deal with them: food, television, sex, drugs, sleep, alcohol, shutting down/avoidance, shopping, anger, reading, getting support from friends or others? Were those coping methods helpful or not helpful?

Do you feel satisfied with your personal life?

What top five values or characteristics do you most value in life (examples: integrity, love, success, money, friendship, support, freedom, etc.)? Please list them in order of importance to you, number one being of the highest importance:

1.

2.

3.

4.

5.

Are you more of an optimist or pessimist? How does that effect your life?

What do you think most about often?

Are your thoughts happy, stressful, sad, etc.?

What would you like to be different, better or more in the 'mental system' of your life (thoughts, thought patterns, thought habits and self-perceptions)?

When you have thoughts about yourself what are they? When you look in the mirror what do you usually think?

How often do you learn new things through reading, researching, taking classes or seminars or having discussions with others?

When you spend time thinking about you and your life, what feelings (either physically or emotionally) do you feel afterwards (examples: anxious, stressed, happy, positive, hopeful, empowered, helpless, out of control, sick to stomach, headache, exhaustion, overwhelmed, or neutral)?

What are your spiritual beliefs?

Do you have any negative association to any spiritual or religious experiences you have had in the past?

How do you choose to practice your beliefs?

How often do you pray? How often do you meditate?

How do you think your spiritual life could be strengthened?

What would you like to be different, better or more in your spiritual life?

What are your five most important spiritual goals (examples: feeling a connection to a higher power, doing more charitable work, reading and studying spiritual materials, or whatever you define as your way of taking action in your spiritual life)?

What are your five most important physical goals (health and anything in your external environment such as finances, home, organization)?

What are your five most important emotional goals (attitudes, emotions, relationships)?

What are your five most important mental goals (thoughts, perceptions, attitudes)?

Transform • Rachel Eva

WEEK

1

SELF DISCOVERY & WELLNESS PLANNING

During your first week you will deep dive into the lessons and the assignments within this program. You can do this entire program on your own, however if you are doing that I *highly* recommend finding a friend who can do the program with you and/or be a supportive and loving accountability partner. Share with them what this program is about and ask if you can give weekly updates of your growth and progress. Ask if they will hold you accountable to your plan and action steps.

As you approach this work and embark on this journey of growth and transformation I encourage you to be fearless and play at 100 percent!

If you miss an assignment, need more time to marinate on the topic or simply don't have enough time for it, *do not give it up forever.* Come back to that assignment later. Finishing the exercises from Week One in Week Six will still bring growth. Do what you can, do your best—whatever that looks like for you, day-to-day!

AWARENESS, ACCEPTANCE & INTENTIONAL ACTION

The three As—awareness, acceptance, action—and action done with intention, are presented below as separate, yet equal components of this program. As you read the following section, take some time to deeply contemplate the questions.

AWARENESS

How many times have you been very aware of your negative thought patterns, self-image, negative habits, beliefs and perceptions? You may not be aware or have connected your patterns with the outcomes you are experiencing in your life. You can't consciously take action on something you are unaware of; it is therefore important to connect the dots.

ACCEPTANCE

This means acceptance of your own responsibility for yourself. You reach empowerment by accepting responsibility for your life, well-being and wellness. Wholeness and balance in all areas of your life is up to you. It is not dependent upon people, places, situations or things outside of you. You are in control of your own mind and the results of the thoughts and beliefs you have. You are in control of your perceptions and your outcomes.

INTENTIONAL ACTION

It is critical to first adopt this belief before any action steps are taken. It is hard for you to take effective action if you are still making statements like:

"I can't help thinking negatively about _____ because they did/do _____."

"I have a bad self-image because my father always told me I was _____."

Whatever you believe about yourself, that belief is a limit you alone have set. What if you are more than that belief? If you change your beliefs, it will change your life. You have the ability to overcome limiting beliefs and to put new beliefs in place. This first requires you to look honestly and fearlessly at your beliefs and your 'stories' about yourself, people and the rest of the world.

Dive deep into your self-discovery; it is amazing what you may find that is holding you back and keeping you from wellness, wholeness and balance in your life. Once you have uncovered these beliefs and stories, ask yourself:

"Who or what would I be without this belief or without this story?"

"What could I be free to do or be?"

"Is this belief or story really true?"

"Does this story or belief serve me in living the life I want or does it limit me?"

"Can I let go of this belief or story if it doesn't serve me?"

No matter what you have learned through popular culture about who you are and what your value is only *you* get to decide what you agree with and what is true for you. No matter what you may have understood through your relationship patterns or the rules of your religion; no matter what you have been told by family members, lovers, teachers or authority figures about who you were and what your value is... you can let go of any of the beliefs or stories that do not serve you! You are uniquely you and no one else can be you. Even your mistakes or the damaging things you've encountered in life do not define you. Those things provide valuable feedback that you can learn from. When you learn from and then learn to let go of your stories, limiting beliefs, negative emotions and patterns you create the best version of yourself the way *you and you alone* envision that to be.

One person's perception is that person's' reality. Since you can let go of old stories and create new perceptions, you can create the life we want. You are free to define yourself and your life.

What definitions, perceptions or stories have you adopted that may not be true or that may not serve you well in being who you desire to be? I once coached a client who was physically unhealthy and had numerous injuries and issues with their body. They spent a lot of time talking about all the things they were: weak, fat, unhealthy, a victim of injury and in pain. I offered a new perspective; one where they could recognize their "inner athlete" or the part inside that held the desire and dedication to overcome the negative self-image. The person chose to adopt it. The paradigm shift—or, that person's new story—gave them the power to completely shift their health status. The client viewed themself as an athlete and started treating their body accordingly with the way they fed and exercised it. The result? Their health began yielding the same results an athlete's health would produce.

This story may seem simplistic yet, subtle shifts in perception greatly affect all areas of the self: mentally, emotionally, physically and spiritually. By stepping out of the victim mentality and into empowerment, my client saw positive change in every area of life.

EXERCISES

There are a few exercises described below. One is time spent in even more self-discovery; one involves nutrition; one is about journaling and one is about creating an action plan. All should be considered ongoing practices—integrate them as daily patterns in your journey of integrative wellness and wholeness.

SELF-DISCOVERY

Talk about or write about what you discovered about yourself and your life by answering the questions in the Self Discovery Form. Focus on your personal history. Get clear about the choices, thoughts and patterns you have been participating in during your life and what results they are creating. Journal in the space provided below:

SELF-SURVEYS

You cannot take action on what you are not aware of; I know this from personal experience.

I walked around with a cloud of frustration hanging all around me. I was unclear, unhappy and unfocused on solutions for a long, long time. I looked everywhere and anywhere outside of myself to feel relief. I turned to relationships, work, eating, shopping and other forms of avoidance. What I truly needed was to heal, grow and learn what it was that I really needed. It was only when I was able to dive into self-discovery with an honest desire for wellness, purpose and wholeness that I developed the willingness to be bold, honest and fearless. When journaling and taking honest self-surveys I was able to see where the outer manifestations of bigger, deeper inner core problems were rooted.

To grow into your best self and wellness in all areas of your life, you must first identify your patterns and roadblocks that separate you from being and acting aligned with your true self.

Here's how self-surveys work: write the food, how much and when you ate. It's best not to be obsessive, so please do not measure for more than a few weeks. You'll be able to see your patterns in a clear way by then. Keep notes or mini journal entries to track of your health status, spiritual life, energy levels, moods, emotions, thoughts, attitudes, sleep and dreams, exercise, and other body functions (bloating, bowel movements, digestive issues, aches or pains, wellness records like a chiropractic appointments, etc.).

HERE'S AN EXAMPLE:

DATE: *January 1, 2015*

NOTES: *Slept 7 hours. Woke up tired. Had to drink large coffee to get moving. Energy ok after. Prayed and tried to practice relaxed breathing on the way to work. Felt connected to God. Started getting tired around 3pm, had another coffee. Got a slight headache at 5pm. Started getting cranky. Had some negative thoughts and self-talk. Did cardio on the treadmill for 20 minutes. Noticed energy increase after. Went to bed at 11pm. Read and tried to meditate but only made it a few minutes.*

SPIRITUAL: *Meditated, did breath work and prayed. Set an intention for the day to focus on the positive things in my life and be grateful.*

ACTION STEPS: *I reached out to an old friend and asked her to forgive me.*

TODAY'S VICTORIES AND CHALLENGES: *Struggled with negative thoughts. The victory was that I didn't get totally caught up in them and let them ruin my day.*

FOOD, DRINKS AND EXERCISE:

1ST MEAL: *7 am — apple, protein shake and ½ cup oatmeal.*

2ND MEAL: *9 am — coffee w/almond milk and stevia, egg white omelette (5 egg whites) with spinach, mushrooms and tomatoes and 2 pieces of whole wheat toast.*

3RD MEAL: *11 am — banana, protein shake and a handful of almonds.*

4TH MEAL: *1pm – 4 oz. grilled chicken, 4 cups mixed salad with 2 tablespoons of vinaigrette dressing and a medium sweet potato. Drank 1/2 gallon of water, three coffees and exercised for a total of 20 minutes.*

On the next page is your wellness journal outline. You may choose to recreate this in another journal (one that might be easier to carry with you) or keep your entries within this book (there are spaces for each weeks Wellness Journal entries at the end of each week in this program). You may be reviewing it and referring to it along the way, so it is important to keep it close by if you are not doing your Wellness Journal entries within this book. It will be a huge resource and roadmap to your growth!

WELLNESS JOURNAL

A wellness journal is one of the most useful tools to use in your self-development process. It provides a place for you to communicate your thoughts and feelings as well as record action steps, results and outcomes of this program's steps. The journal is a great place for you to check on your internal landscape, connect with your four body systems and write about what you discover through 'self-survey.'

It's important for your mental, emotional, physical and spiritual systems to keep a wellness journal. It gives you a place to communicate with yourself freely and safely, and it acts as a reference guide, a resource and a tool for planning, achieving, expanding and creating new goals. It is proven that people who track their action steps are more successful at achieving goals and creating new habits that allow for success!

As a part of this program you write in a journal *daily*. Some Wellness Journal entries will be longer; some shorter, or may even be only a few sentences. Be consistent with your journaling—it shows its worth shortly after you begin!

Day # _____   Date: _____

Notes:

Today I set an intention of:

In today's meditation I noticed:

Action steps:

Today's victories and challenges:

Food, drinks, exercise & self care:

Today's actions, thoughts & experiences in the mental, emotional, physical & spiritual systems:

BALANCE
ACTION GRAPH/ACTION PLAN:

Taking information from your Self-Discovery Form as well as your own thoughts and feedback, fill in the Action Graph below. This will become your Wellness Action Plan.

ACTION GRAPH

PROBLEM OR ISSUE IDENTIFIED (Example: Want to be in a relationship)	WHAT ABOUT IT IS A PROBLEM? (Example: I feel sad and lonely)	STEPS ALREADY TAKEN TO TRY TO RESOLVE IT (Example: Talked about it with my friends)	ADDITIONAL STEP I CAN TAKE (Example: Join an online dating site)

ACTION GRAPH

PROBLEM OR ISSUE IDENTIFIED	WHAT ABOUT IT IS A PROBLEM?	STEPS ALREADY TAKEN TO TRY TO RESOLVE IT	ADDITIONAL STEP I CAN TAKE

PERSONALITY TESTS
& SELF DISCOVERY TOOLS

Personality tests such as the DISC, Myers-Briggs, Enneagram and also *The Five Love Languages* are very helpful tools in self-discovery. Personality tests give valuable feedback to understanding how you 'tick' and what moving towards balance means for *you*. For example, an introvert moving towards balance will call for very a very different action plan than an extrovert. I recommend that you take a personality test as well as read and do *The Five Love Languages* (to discover the way you most feel loved/supported and also express love/support), as it will help increase the effectiveness of all the work you in this program. Most of these are available for free online.

YOUR PERSONALITY & COMMUNICATION STYLE

Discovering more about your unique design and the way you communicate is a tremendous tool for growth and clarity! Your personality type and the way you express and receive love are areas of self-discovery you can unpack through tools like the Enneagram, Myers-Briggs, DISC and the book *The Five Love Languages*.

The Enneagram is a personality typing system that consists of nine different types. Everyone is considered to be one single type, although one can have traits belonging to other ones. The Enneagram personality test is helpful in both understanding yourself as well as gaining deeper clarity on how to communicate, work with and be in relationships with other types. For a free self-test or more information, search the internet.

According to their web site, The Myers Briggs Type Indicator® (MBTI®) is an introspective self-report questionnaire designed to indicate psychological preferences in how people perceive the world and make decisions. The MBTI® was constructed by Katharine Cook Briggs and her daughter Isabel Briggs Myers. It is based on the typological theory proposed by Carl Jung who had speculated that there are four principal psychological functions by which humans experience the world: sensation, intuition, feeling, and thinking. One of these four functions is dominant for a person most of the time. The MBTI® was constructed for normal populations and emphasizes the value of naturally occurring differences. To take the test online visit: Capt.org/take-mbti-assessment/mbti.htm. Or for more detailed information about the Myers Briggs visit: MyersBriggs.org/my-mbti-personality-type/take-the-mbti-instrument/.

The DISC profile is a personality test that helps to learn your strengths and weaknesses in order to grow, live and function in the areas of your strengths. More information and tests are available at: DiscProfile.com.

Identify your specific love language through the book *The Five Love Languages* by Gary Chapman or by visiting their website. Everyone has a primary love language that you speak, express in your actions and understand. It is the primary way you communicate love to the people you care about and the way that you most desire love to be communicated to you by those you care about. It is also an important tool for discovering the things that make you feel appreciated and acknowledged in every one of your relationships.

From the list and description of each of the five love languages below, please identify your primary and secondary love language (how you feel most loved and appreciated), then determine the primary and secondary love languages of the people who you are closest to in life. Practice expressing love and appreciation to these people using *their* primary love language. Example; if you identify that your mother's love language is words of affirmation, send her a card filled with words about how special and loved she is.

Actions don't always speak louder than words. If "words" are your love language, unsolicited compliments mean the world to you. Hearing the words, "I love you," is important—hearing the reasons behind that love sends your spirits skyward. Insults can leave you shattered and are not easily forgotten.

If "quality time" is your love language, nothing says "I love you," like full, undivided attention. Being there for this type of person is critical, but really being there—with the TV off, fork and knife down, and all chores and tasks on standby—makes your significant other feel truly special and loved. Distractions, postponed dates, or the failure to listen can be especially hurtful.

Don't mistake the "receiving gifts" love language for materialism; the receiver of gifts thrives on the love, thoughtfulness, and effort behind the gift. If you speak this language, the perfect gift or gesture shows that you are known, you are cared for, and you are prized above whatever was sacrificed to bring the gift to you. A missed birthday, anniversary, or a hasty, thoughtless gift would be disastrous—so would the absence of everyday gestures in the form of simple gifts.

Acts of service is another form of love language. Can vacuuming the floors really be an expression of love? Absolutely! Anything you do to ease the burden of responsibilities weighing on an "acts of service" person will speak volumes. The words he or she most wants to hear are: "Let me do that for you." Laziness, broken commitments, and making more work for them tell speakers of this language their feelings don't matter.

The love language of physical touch isn't all about the bedroom or intimate touch. A person whose primary love language is physical touch is very 'touchy.' Hugs, pats on the back, holding hands, and thoughtful touches on the arm, shoulder, or face can all be ways to show excitement, concern, care and love for this kind of person. Physical presence and accessibility are crucial, while neglect or abuse can be unforgivable and destructive.

These excerpts are all from 5LoveLanguages.com/learn-the-languages/the-five-love-languages/ and you're encouraged to visit this site to learn more.

Now that you've read the material for Week One, here are some testimonials of former students after getting through the first week's assignments and exercises:

"This week was hard because I'd been hiding a lot of truths about myself from myself and this work shed a lot of light in areas I kept in darkness. My favorite aspect of the program was the meditations. I spend so much time in my head that I really enjoyed engaging my body spiritually and mentally. I know that sounds weird but as I've gained weight over the years, I've literally had a mental disassociation with my body since it's a reminder of the bad choices I've made. So while I inhabit it, I hadn't felt fully integrated with it. Doing meditations helped me reconnect all the pieces and start a full healing process."
~ Gabrielle

"The self-discovery process in week one helped me be still and evaluate myself and my journey."
~ Reyna

"Week One had a LOT of information. I was a little sad to discover how low my opinion of myself was, but I was very encouraged by the tools provided to work my way out of that."
~ Jessika

NOTES:

Transform • Rachel Eva

Transform • Rachel Eva

Transform • Rachel Eva

WEEK 2

WHO ARE WE? WHAT ARE OUR STORIES?

Your words and thoughts are powerful. They are like seeds that fall upon the soil and when you water them, they grow into reality. The thoughts and words you repeat turn into the actions you take. Those actions lead you somewhere. The question is: are they leading you where you want to go?

Many people have had seeds that were rooted in limiting beliefs and perceptions about who they were, what they were capable of and what the world around them was like. It is important to learn how to see yourself and your world in a way that empowers you to grow into your truest, fullest self in ALL areas of your life and in all four systems; mental, emotional, physical and spiritual.

We all have 'stories' that are the way we view our past, who we are, our strengths, our weaknesses, our personal history and how we project our vision of our future. Our stories are made up of the definitions and labels we assign or believe in about ourselves, others and the world. Let go of your stories and beliefs that limit you. With intention, plant seeds that will allow and promote you to grow into the best versions of yourself.

It is so easy to fall into the cycle of judgment and criticism towards yourself, your lives and others. There are so many images and cultural opinions being launched at you constantly that tell you what success, prosperity, health and happiness look like. Subconsciously they can creep in and begin to form your thoughts and definition of self, others and the world.

When you notice negative judgments, negative thoughts and limiting beliefs sneaking into your thought life, it is time to *pump the brakes* and stop getting into agreement with those thoughts! Each person is in control of their mind and their life. What you do in your mind, both consciously and unconsciously, manifests outwardly through actions and things you create and attract.

HABITS, VALUES & PATTERNS

Your habits and patterns should reflect your values but sometimes that doesn't happen.

Your values are the things that are important to you. Each of your values has a different priority level or order of importance. Your values should not be in conflict with each other and your habits and patterns also should be congruent or true to your values. If they aren't you are not being true to yourself and you are acting in conflict. In that case, an internal battle (both consciously and unconsciously) will create negative results in all four of your systems as well as in every major area of your life.

How ever you define your values, do not correct or pass judgment on them or yourself. Aim to discover if they are effective values for you to achieve the things you want within your life and if they will promote wholeness in all four systems. Only you can define your values and determine if they are effective.

Habits are behaviors you repeat that eventually become automatic and are defined as a usual way of behaving; something that a person does often in a regular and repeated way.

Patterns are a group or series of habits that you repeat and eventually become an unconscious design you follow. Patterns can also be defined as: a repeated form or design, especially to decorate something; the regular and repeated way in which something happens or is done; something that happens in a regular and repeated way. I particularly like the definition of a pattern as a 'repeated form or design used to decorate something'. This is a beautiful analogy for how people 'decorate' or design their lives. It expresses individual responsibility and power to create the life you want versus being victims of circumstance.

EXERCISES

The following exercises are meant to get you to a state of clear thinking—for yourself and to help you identify any beliefs you may be limiting you. When your thoughts become clear and free from limiting beliefs, you will be guided towards effective actions that lead towards resolving issues, achieving goals and experiencing the things you want to experience in your life.

Read through the steps listed in the exercise category below. Give the concepts some deep thought—allow yourself some time to sit in a quiet place and just think! When you're ready, write about your experience of thinking about your thoughts in your wellness journal. Use the lists as your guide for writing; if possible, write on all the points in order to get a clear overview of the current status of your four systems: mental, emotional, physical and spiritual.

DEFINITIONS OF SELF BY SELF, WORLD & ENVIRONMENT

'Know thyself' is a phrase that might be as old as time yet it never came with instructions! Here are the steps to knowing yourself as you are in this present moment and in this particular era of your life. To discover your definitions and beliefs I pose these questions to you and recommend that you answer each from your perspective of what is true NOW and what has been true in the PAST versus what you WANT the answer to be in the future.

1. How would you describe your physical self, emotional self, mental self and spiritual self?

_____

_____

_____

_____

2. How would guess that your friends would describe you?

_____

_____

_____

_____

3. How would guess that your family would describe you?

4. How would you guess that your boss, co-workers or business associates would describe you?

5. How would you guess that your neighbors and people in your community would describe you?

6. By the world's standards, describe how you believe you 'measure up' to its expectations.

7. By your family members' standards, describe how you think you 'measure up' to their expectations.

_____
_____
_____
_____

8. Are these true?

_____
_____
_____
_____

9. Who would I be or who could I be without these thoughts/beliefs?

_____
_____
_____
_____

10. Fill in the blank: I should be more _____.

11. Fill in the blank: I want to be more _____.

12. Fill in the blank: I should be less _____.

13. Fill in the blank: I want to be less _____.

14. Are those true?

15. Who would I be or who could I be without these thoughts/beliefs?

Once you have discovered your self-perception, whether it stemmed from messages you heard or saw, you have chosen to agree with these and implement them or act upon them as if they were true. Invite yourself to journal on how you would like to redefine yourself and also what definitions of self would promote wholeness and achieving your goals.

Now that you've addressed your picture or perception of yourself, clarity of mind on these four points is essential:

1. Beliefs (the things/definitions/opinions/thoughts/ideas you have chosen to agree to).

2. Definitions (how you define things like success, love, happiness, freedom).

3. Values (what is important to you).

4. Models of the world (your perception of the world and how it works).

NEXT, YOU'LL BRING INTENTIONALITY TO MEET YOUR CLARITY BY:

1. Consciously re-defining your definitions of the words you use to describe the concepts that are most important to you.
2. Consciously re-assessing beliefs and belief systems on which you have based your life.
3. Putting your top values in order of importance..
4. Reframing your model of the world to expand your options for a new, better reality.
5. Processing and releasing negative emotions and attachments.

TAKING EFFECTIVE ACTIONS THAT LEAD TO ACHIEVING YOUR GOALS IS DONE BY:

1. Determining new actions that can be taken based on your new beliefs, definitions, values and models of the world.
2. Examining current patterns and habits and determining if they align with your new intentional frameworks.
3. Making adjustments in patterns and habits through writing an action plan.

Once you have gotten clarity on your beliefs and values, it is time to take action steps towards balance. Here are some simple action steps to take that move you towards balance:

1. Face any of your negative feelings. This means to see them in a clear way, feel them and also consciously choose not to magnify them and then release them. We DO need to feel our feelings. Processing and releasing negative emotions is critical. Acknowledge them, feel them, release them and then shift your focus.
2. Become conscious of your thought life. Observe the places and feelings where your mind and thoughts drift to. Notice the patterns. Notice where and what you spend the majority of your thought life invested in or on.
3. Notice what emotions and physical sensations result from your thoughts.
4. Meditate on your values and beliefs to see and uncover core issues; where your thought patterns are rooted and arise from.
5. Ask yourself if the thoughts are *true*; are they fact or based on your opinion, your experience, your perception and perspective?
6. Ask yourself: "Are these patterns, root issues, beliefs and/or values serving me well now? If no, can I let go of them and choose to replace them with ones that will lead to the results I want?"

CREATING YOUR OVERALL WELLNESS PLAN

Everyone's life is unique, and as you create your own unique wellness plan it is great to have a template that you can use. Using all of the information you brought to the surface of your awareness through doing the Self Discovery Form and Action Graph Exercise you will fill out the sections below to get specific and clear about actions you can take, this will become your overall wellness plan. It is important to take steps towards bringing balance to all four systems; mental, emotional, physical and spiritual as well as steps to bring balance to each of the major areas of your life; career, finances, family, relationships, health, self development and spirituality.

MY WELLNESS PLAN ACTION STEPS

Using what you discovered in the Action Graph Exercise write out the tasks or steps to put into action in each area below. These are steps you want to take to move you from where you are towards where you want to be. Do not be concerned at the moment about when or how often you will do these things—just list them in the appropriate section below:

Health Action Plan (steps to take towards more wellness and balance in my health - *always consult your doctor before starting or changing a fitness or nutrition program!):

1. _____

2.

3.

4.

5.

NUTRITION

Read the "Under Six Nutrition" and "The Balanced Plate" material below. These nutrition plans are designed to help you become aware of how to bring your nutrition into more balance. I recommend trying to follow both, however please do so in a balanced manor! Doing 10 percent is better then doing 0 percent. Remember to listen to your own body over any outside recommendations, including my own.

UNDER SIX NUTRITION

This may be the simplest nutrition plan to eat in a clean and toxic free way! The concept is that all your foods (meals) should be made up of recipes (not prepared meals but cooked at home by you) that have six or less ingredients in them (not including clean seasonings like Himalayan salt, garlic, fresh green herbs such as oregano, cilantro, parsley etc.). The six ingredients should all be whole foods (a single food such as a pepper versus a can of peppers that also have other preservatives and ingredients in it); made up of one ingredient that is fresh, not frozen or canned or boxed. That's it. Have your meals home cooked and made up of six (or less) whole food ingredients or items!

THE BALANCED PLATE NUTRITION PLAN

'All Things in Balance' is the motto I live by and recommend, so I created The Balanced Plate Nutrition Plan. If you are overwhelmed by the plethora of information on how to eat healthy and how much, start by creating a new approach to your nutritional intake. Eat more times through out the day, have smaller meals with each composed as a 'balanced plate' (see graphic below with the protein, denser carbohydrates, green vegetables and healthy fat portion break down), drink more water, avoid eating at restaurants (not ALWAYS, but mostly), and avoid pre-cooked/pre-prepared foods.

The 'balanced plate' concept for each meal is shown below; this gives you a visual guide. The exact breakdown (in case you're a numbers person) is that one half of the plate holds raw or lightly cooked green vegetables; one fourth of the plate is lean (not fatty) protein such as fish or white meat chicken; one fourth of the plate is clean, low-glycemic carbohydrates (examples are: sweet potato, beans, black rice). Add one heaping tablespoon of a healthy fat source (examples are: nuts, coconut or olive oil and avocado), and you'll have a 'balanced plate!' However, please listen to your own body versus counting calories, weighing food or following my sizes. Your body may need larger or smaller portions in each meal. However no matter what your total portion size is, break it down by having ½ of the total meal as green veggies, ¼ of the total meal as dense low-glycemic carbohydrates, ¼ of the total meal as lean protein and about 1 tablespoon to 1 ounce of healthy fats.

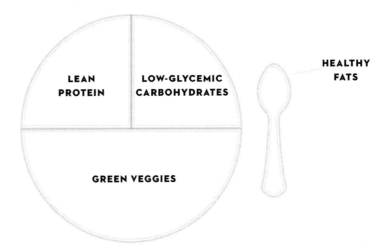

The 'balanced plate' and the 'under 6' are a great place to begin a lifelong practice of good nutrition for yourself. Add or subtract amounts based on what you feel your body needs—just add or subtract in the same balance (add an equal amount to all areas or take away a small amount from all areas).

NUTRITION PLAN
(STEPS TO TAKE TO EAT HEALTHIER & BE HEALTHIER)

Areas to move towards balance:

Action steps to take:

FITNESS

Every body and every unique personality has different needs for an exercise program. What you enjoy and will be able to sustain time and energy wise will be very different from someone else's fitness. Give yourself permission to develop and experiment with implementing a balanced fitness plan. See what works for you and how your body responds as well as what does not work. When you create your fitness plan try to make choices that address bringing the fitness level and physical body into more balance with the following elements; cardiovascular and endurance building exercise, stretching and restorative exercises as well as strengthening and toning exercises.

Which specific exercises, workouts or classes that you choose will take some research and trail and error on your part. My main recommendation is play, experiment and make choices that even when challenging are fun!

WEEKLY FITNESS PLAN
(STEPS TO TAKE TO BE FIT & STRONG IN MY BODY)

After considering what your personal needs are in this area and how to achieve them, write your fitness plan in below for *each* area of your body. It's about *whole* person wellness:

Cardiovascular health and endurance exercises:

_____

_____

_____

_____

_____

Stretching and restorative exercises:

Strengthening and toning exercises:

CAREER & FINANCE ACTION PLAN
(STEPS TO TAKE TO MOVE MY CAREER AND FINANCES FROM WHERE THEY ARE NOW TOWARDS WHERE I WANT THEM TO BE):

Areas to move towards balance:

Action steps to take:

EMOTIONAL ACTION PLAN: FAMILY & RELATIONSHIPS

These are the steps you will take to improve your relationships. Your emotions, when balanced, will allow you to experience greater joy. You can only change a relationship by changing yourself.

Areas to move towards balance:

Action steps to take:

SPIRITUAL ACTION PLAN

Areas to move towards balance:

Action steps to take:

WEEKLY TO DO LIST FOR SELF-CARE

Here you will create a weekly 'to do list' that includes addressing the needs of all four systems: mental, emotional, physical and spiritual. Once you have written your weekly to do list, take a good look at your schedule and begin a daily exercise of writing your overall wellness plan as a daily 'to do' list as well.

Things I will do in the next week to take care of myself mentally, physically, emotionally and spiritually:

1.
2.
3.
4.
5.
6.
7.
8.
9.
10.

WRITE DOWN YOUR STORIES

What are the stories that no longer serve you? What are the beliefs you have agreed with or adopted that are leading you away from wholeness and wellness in your life?

NOTES:

Transform • Rachel Eva

Transform • Rachel Eva

Transform • Rachel Eva

WEEK 3

FINDING YOUR TRUTH, WELLNESS & BALANCE

Somewhere along the way we all learn the things we now know or unconsciously act upon. Some of those things currently work for us and some don't. Instead of judging them as right or wrong, I invite you to consider them as effective or non-effective for *you*. What is effective for you during one time in your life may not be effective in another time. All negative patterns, limiting beliefs and definitions were helpful in some way or else you wouldn't have chosen to agree with them and act on them.

Give yourself permission to uncover and discover what is true for you. What is helpful to you in the area of growing? What is helpful to you in creating what you want in the areas of health, career, finances, relationships, family, self-development and spirituality? This is *your* life; no one else is living in your shoes. You are responsible for creating the life you desire. You are responsible for your outcomes, so this means *you* get to decide what will lead you where you want to go.

Sometimes this takes experimenting with choices. You may decide to try out a specific fitness or nutrition plan, a specific career or relationship path, only to discover it wasn't effective for you. That's OK! That is living life! You can always choose a new path based on the learnings. It's OK to course correct!

Understanding your season of life and how to honor it is another important part of the journey towards wellness, balance and wholeness in all areas of your life. Discovering what *you* connect with or what works best for you in the midst of the specific season you are in is hugely helpful. It is important to be taking steps towards wellness, wholeness and balance that *you* are congruent with. Again, what works for one person may not work best for another. Honor your path. And honor the paths of others with a heart full of compassion!

Week three offers you a way to map your values along with meditation and breath techniques to calm and center you. When you are calm and centered, the pace of your life becomes more luxurious and enjoyable. Meditation is also a simple way to increase wellness in all four systems; mental, emotional, physical and spiritual.

LISTING YOUR VALUES

Fill in the blanks with each of your top values within each major area of life. Put them in order of importance, 1 being most important and 10 less important. These are your top 10 values within each area:

Career:

1.
2.
3.
4.
5.
6.
7.
8.
9.
10.

Family:

1.
2.
3.
4.
5.
6.
7.
8.
9.
10.

Relationships: Romantic relationships/partner and friends:

1.
2.
3.
4.
5.
6.
7.
8.
9.
10.

Health and fitness:

1.
2.
3.
4.
5.
6.
7.
8.
9.
10.

Self-development:

1.
2.
3.
4.
5.
6.
7.
8.
9.
10.

Spirituality:

1.
2.
3.
4.
5.
6.
7.
8.
9.
10.

Now take a look at all of the major life areas top ten values and journal below on what aspects of each major area of your life may currently be in direct conflict with your values. Also write down some ideas as to what you can add, change or remove in these areas that will allow you to be more aligned with your top values.

MEDITATION

Let's dive into how *specifically* to begin meditating. As meditation has become more and more popular over the years, different forms of meditation have blossomed throughout the world and in the United States' culture. There are many different meditation techniques. Here is a very simple beginner's meditation.

Meditation can be effective if done for 1 minute or an hour, so meditate for however long you feel serves you best.

Begin sitting in a quiet and comfortable space where you will be uninterrupted. Close your eyes and focus your attention on your breath, drawing each breath in, all the way down to the base of your belly, feeling your belly expand with oxygen and feeling your belly withdraw as you release your breath fully on the exhale, and just begin focusing your attention on (or watching; paying attention to) breathing in and out naturally, and deeply.

Continue nice, deep, full breath cycles.

As you do this, if any thoughts come into your mind as distractions, lovingly acknowledge them and release them. Do this by imagining that you're putting the thought inside of a box, and placing the box up on a shelf. You can come back after the meditation and take the box off the shelf and dive into that thought if you wish. For now, you don't want to get involved in, or in a relationship, with any thoughts, simply be. If your mind drifts, bring your attention back to your breath, allowing every part of your body and mind to become still, and simply continue this focused breathing for as long as you would like to stay in a state of quiet meditation.

I invite you to take a moment now and just sit back and experience that meditation practice within your body. If you want to view a video example or learn more tools for meditation I offer audio and video options on my web site at RachelEvaOnline.com

BREATHING TECHNIQUES

Breathing techniques are another form of a stress reduction practice. They are effective in reducing stress on the physiological level, and the cellular level, within the body. If you experience stress, tension, anxiety or mental health issues like depression, these breathing techniques, or exercises, will be beneficial.

The first breath technique is called the "Ha Breath," or "Ha Breathing." The second breathing technique is called "Belly Breath," and then the third technique is to put both the "Ha Breath" and the "Belly Breath" together. You can use the "Ha Breath" by itself, the "Belly Breath" by itself or the combination—all together.

A good use of the "Ha Breath" by itself is as a pause button. When you're facing a stressful, frustrating, emotionally hurtful situation, using "Ha Breath" puts a stop to the situation and releases the tension. A good time to use the "Belly Breath" by itself is when you are processing a negative emotion. What does this mean? If you are experiencing a negative emotion that you would normally want to shut down, avoid and not face, using the "Belly Breath" lets you move through the negative emotion without suppressing it. A great time to use both in combination is when you really need to reset, release and redirect both your emotions and thoughts.

"HA BREATH" TECHNIQUE

The "Ha Breath" is a very simple, very fast pause-and-release technique. Simply take a deep inhale through your nose, drawing breath all the way down into your belly, then opening your mouth and sigh out the air as you are exhaling. It sounds like "Haaaaaaaaaa." I suggest that you do this any time you wish and especially at the first sign of stress, tension, or negative emotions like anger or frustration, or anxiety.

BELLY BREATH

Begin the "Belly Breath" by sitting in a comfortable position. Place your hands on your belly. Breathe in deep down to feel your belly expand up against your hands. And, as you exhale, fully releasing all of the air, getting all of the breath out of your body, you should feel your hands moving with your belly as it contracts. Again inhale, drawing the breath all the way down into the belly; exhale. It's as simple as that. The "Belly Breath" can be done in just a few minutes. Even taking five or six belly breaths in a row can have a good effect on all four systems because it helps release stress.

MERGING THE TWO BREATH TECHNIQUES

Do three "Ha Breaths" and then shift the focus into one minute of belly breathing. This is a fantastic exercise for people who suffer from anxiety. Here is how it looks: Ha Breath. Ha Breath. Ha Breath. Bring your hands to your belly and begin the "Belly Breath." Deeply inhale, drawing breath all the way down to the base of your belly, then exhale fully releasing all of the air. Repeat. Continue this "Belly Breath" for one full minute. That's it. Now you have combined the two breath techniques into a third.

Transform • Rachel Eva

NOTES:

Transform • Rachel Eva

Transform • Rachel Eva

Transform • Rachel Eva

WEEK 4

TIME & HEART MANAGEMENT

Managing your needs and desires in order to create success in all areas of your life means you have to get intentional. It's easy to get caught up in all of your 'must do' items and completely ignore yourself and your own needs. You must learn to put *your* needs first. How can you give away what you don't have to give?

A friend told me about a remarkable woman she'd known. The woman lived through the Second World War in Europe as a child. She then got a job that turned into a career as a one of the top people in a large company. She got married and raised three children while she continued to work—and stay married! At the end of her life, my friend asked her what she would have changed over the course of her lifetime and experiences. After some quiet consideration, this woman said, "I would have taken more time for myself. I was busy, but I was also smart. I should have figured out a way! My life was good, but it could have been so much better."

Look at time like it's a bank...and you are the account. If the bank is on empty, or even worse in overdraft (in the negative) the bank account is useless! It takes *daily* deposits into yourself in order to intentionally create the life you want to live. When you are not intentional with the investment of your time, resources and energy (including emotional energy) you fall prey to living a *reactive* life versus a *proactive* life. A proactive life takes intentional, balanced actions that lead towards wellness in all other areas.

Again I will repeat this powerful message: *get intentional*. Success in any area takes intentionality.

EMOTIONAL GROWTH TECHNIQUES

Western culture has millions of products aimed towards avoiding anything that feels bad, painful and uncomfortable or that is perceived as negative. It has become the norm in popular culture to 'zone out' and 'decompress' by avoiding struggles, challenges or discomforts. When you have a negative emotion in response to something, it is a signal for you to pay attention. You need to *be with it* versus avoid it. How else can you process and release it? If you don't release it, you are shoving it down and covering it up. Your subconscious is still aware of it and all four systems (mental, emotional, physical and spiritual) are affected by it whether you are currently feeling it or not.

In moving towards wholeness in the emotional system it is important to use techniques to process and release negative emotions. This does not mean you immerse yourself and wallow in your feelings. There is a difference between processing and wallowing. Wallowing magnifies your emotional state. Processing is like peeling an onion. With each layer emotions, get recognized and felt; they naturally come up so that you can learn from them and release them.

PRESERVE THE LEARNINGS

It is not uncommon for people to hold onto their negative emotions, both consciously and unconsciously in order to remain connected to the person or situation, or to ensure they don't get into the situation again (this is the 'learning' or lesson from an experience). Example: "If I am no longer sad about his death, then I will no longer be connected to him. He will really be gone." Another example: "If I let go of fear then I might not be able to protect myself from being assaulted again."

When you preserve the learnings, you can become ready to release negative emotions. Figuring out on a conscious level what you can learn, or, what you need to learn from those circumstances that caused the negative emotions, is an important assignment to give yourself. Meditating on the question "What is the learning or lesson?" can be a powerful step towards wholeness in the emotional system.

RELEASING NEGATIVE EMOTIONS

Healthy processing or grieving of negative emotions and unmet expectations are a part of the emotional wellness process. There are many release techniques and it's about finding the one that resonates best with you. There are techniques this curriculum teaches and a plethora more out there in the world. Discovering effective release techniques is a beautiful path to emotional wellness and should begin with a few simple questions:

1. How do you think you release or let go of emotional baggage best?
2. Has anything you have done before or heard of doing feel like an effective choice for you in releasing negative emotions?
3. When you experience a negative emotion, what do you tend to do to deal with it?
4. Do you feel the way you are currently dealing with negative emotions is helpful in processing them, getting the learning or lesson and then releasing them?

ARTISTIC PROCESS & RELEASE TECHNIQUE

The Artistic Process and Release Technique can incorporate anything artistic, anything creative that you connect with such as music, painting, singing or any other artistic expression that you feel moves or inspires you. Here are the steps:

1. Set aside uninterrupted time for 30 to 60 minutes.
2. Set up or prepare for whatever artistic expression is going to take place. If it is art, set out paints, a canvas, paint brushes. If it's music, get an instrument out; if singing then playing music to sing along with. Step 2 is preparing the creative space.
3. Set an intention for the exercise. For example: "My intention is to process the sadness about _____ and release it."
4. Get associated to or connected with the feeling that you want to process and release. This looks like simply taking a few quiet moments to think about and reflect upon the negative

emotion and the circumstances attached to it.
5. Let it flow and let it go. As that emotion rises within you, allow yourself to feel it and begin participating in the artistic expression that you have chosen. Let your emotions flow and let them go through you, and out of you through the artistic expression. Paint the feeling. Sing the feeling out, or whatever other form of artistic expression you have chosen. Let the emotion flow through you and go out of you through your artistic expression.

And after completing those five steps, it's always very helpful to write about it in your wellness journal later.

Ask yourself the following questions:

1. What did I get out of that experience?
2. What did I learn?
3. What did I process?
4. What did I release?
5. What am I able to now let go of or change?

MOVEMENT PROCESSING & RELEASE

1. Set aside uninterrupted time for 30 to 60 minutes.
2. Set up or prepare for physical movement. This may mean setting up exercise equipment, going to a gym, clearing a space in order to dance, or going to a hiking trail.
3. Set an intention for the exercise. For example: "My intention is to process the fear I am experiencing in relation to _____ and release it."
4. Get associated to or connected to the feeling that you want to process and release. Take a few quiet moments to think about and reflect upon the negative emotion you're wanting to process and release.
5. Let it flow and let it go. As that emotion rises within you, allow yourself to feel it and begin the chosen form of movement. Express the emotion out of your system through the dance, exercise, yoga, hiking, or whatever activity you have chosen. Allow yourself to continue the movement until you feel you have released the negative feeling and you have a sense of relief. Sometimes that even looks like exhaustion, or just feeling like you've emptied yourself out. Remember to keep safety in mind as you do this, for example running on a treadmill while having your eyes closed may be very dangerous. I use that example because I actually did that and the results were less then my desired outcome to say the least! I did get 'the learning' from that and chose to make safe movement a priority in future 'process and release' movement sessions.

BREATHE THROUGH IT

Another technique for processing and releasing negative emotions is using your breath. The technique of Breathe Through It can also called an Emotional Release Meditation. The Breathe Through It technique is different than the other breath techniques—the "Ha Breath" and the "Belly Breath." However, both of those breathing techniques can be merged again into this one.

In the Breathe Through It Technique, you merge focused breath with the specific steps set before in the other two techniques. Here are the steps:
1. Set aside uninterrupted time for 30 to 60 minutes.
2. Set up or prepare a quiet and comfortable space. You may want to light candles, play gentle, soft music in the background, dim the lights or whatever else might feel safe, relaxed and comfortable for you.

3. Set an intention for the exercise. For example: "My intention is to process the disappointment about _____ and release it."
4. Get associated to or connected with the feeling that you want to process and release. Take a few quiet moments to think about and reflect upon the negative emotion you want to process and release.
5. Sitting in a comfortable position, begin a deep breathing exercise. I recommend the "Belly Breath" versus the "Ha Breath" for this specific exercise. As you do the breathing exercise, let it flow and let it go. As that emotion rises within you, feel and be with the emotion, allowing it to flow, resonate and express however it happens. You may experience tears, laughter or absolutely no outer expression. Simply feel the feelings as you continue that deep breath work. And as you breathe, and as you feel, and let the emotion flow, let those feelings go with each exhale. By imagining, with each exhale, the negative emotion is being released from the body, you'll allow yourself to continue that deep breathing pattern until you feel you have released that feeling, and you have a sense of a relief or calmness.

As with all of the other emotional process and release techniques, write about your experience in your wellness journal. This will not only help to learn what you've gotten from this experience, it will also help you to learn how you process and release emotions most effectively in the future. Learning how you best process and release negative emotions is an important step in your self-discovery process and when put into action will lead to growth.

GETTING REAL ABOUT
WHAT YOU ARE IN A RELATIONSHIP WITH

Make a list of where you are spending your energy, time, money, resources and thoughts.

1. _____

2. _____

3. _____

4. _____

5. _____

6. _____

BUDGET

It is important for you to have a budget for success! Create a budget for your finances, investments of energy and a budget for time. There are many different budgeting tools out there that you can use, and you can also use the blank schedule and budget below within the curriculum. The format for budgeting is not as important as getting it down on paper and beginning to implement it in your life.

Here is an example of what a time, energy and resource (money) budget could look like:

Monthly Expenses – (rent, phone, car, gas, food etc.)

Weekly fun money & self care – (eating out, yoga class)

I have energy for going out with friends _____ time per week on the weekend.

I have energy to do something nice for myself for _____ hours each week.

I am allocating $_____ towards my fitness, health and wellness each month.

I will wake up at _____ time during the week and go to sleep at _____ time during the week, this will give me _____ hours of sleep each night.

I have energy for _____ hours of errands each week and I can best do those on _____ (Sunday as an example) day during the week.

I have _____ hours per week to invest in my health and fitness.

My family obligations each week are _____, I can (or can't) do this alone. I need help with

SCHEDULE

Create a weekly schedule that includes actions that are steps towards meeting your goals. Make sure you are creating a realistic, balanced and supportive schedule that allows for time and energy to take care of yourself and your responsibilities.

Monday:

Tuesday:

Wednesday:

Thursday:

Friday:

Saturday:

Sunday:

MIND MAPPING EXERCISE

Mind maps help you to see your life in a visual way. They identify the areas that are balanced or imbalanced and also allows you to add goals with clarity and action steps.

In order to bring balance to your life it is important to do this exercise for all four systems which are defined once again here:

MENTAL: Your thought life, thought patterns, attitudes and beliefs.

EMOTIONAL: Your emotions and relationships with (and towards) yourself and others.

PHYSICAL: Your health, body and anything you have or do not have on the physical level (such as finances, home, car, etc.).

SPIRITUAL: Your connection to your true self, a 'higher power,' to the world and others, as well as your spiritual life and self development.

HERE ARE THE STEPS FOR CREATING A MIND MAP:

1. Get a large piece of paper.
2. Draw four circles on the paper. In one circle, write MENTAL; in the next, write EMOTIONAL; next, PHYSICAL and the last one, SPIRITUAL.
3. Draw 'spokes' or lines off of each circle.
4. On each spoke, write some action that you take currently and also can add to bring balance, wellness and wholeness within that circle's system. Take a look at the current things you do for each system. Think of additional things you can do to bring more balance, wellness and wholeness within that system. Also think of your specific goals in each area (example: build up a nest egg in my savings account).
5. Get a different color pen or pencil then the one you have been using. This color represents goals. Draw a spoke off each system for each goal you have within that system and then write the goal on that line/spoke in the new color.

6. Get a third color pen or pencil. Draw more spokes off each circle/system. In your third color, write the specific action steps you can take within each circle/system to bring more wholeness, wellness and balance.
7. You can add pictures, shapes or any other creative visual way you want to represent the words on the spokes or leave it as is!
8. Put up your mind map on the wall or somewhere you will see it daily. This visual will serve as a daily reminder for you as to what intentions to set for the day and which actions you can take to lead you towards where you want to go.

Here is an example of what your mind map can look like, however, get creative and make it your own. It is just important to visually represent what you want to be moving towards mentally, emotionally, physically and spiritually.

MIND MAP EXAMPLE

SMART GOAL SETTING EXERCISE

What is a SMART goal? It is:

S = Specific and Simple
M = Measurable and Meaningful *to you*
A = Achievable
R = Realistic
T = Timed and Moving TOWARDS what you want

Whenever you set a goal, I recommend taking the following steps to help the goal setting and goal getting be successful:

1. Write out your goal in SMART goal format.
2. Set an intention towards that goal and meditate/visualize what it will be like once it is achieved.
3. Create task lists based on your SMART goal.
4. Take *action* daily!
5. Let go of the outcome. This one can be challenging...there is a difference between wanting a desired outcome and being attached to a desired outcome. Many times things unfold and as they do, they may look different then what you expected. So remain open minded and open hearted as you journey down your path.

NOW, WRITE OUT YOUR GOALS FOR THIS PROGRAM IN SMART GOAL FORMAT:

Goal 1:

S

M

A

R

T

Goal 2:

S

M

A

R

T

Goal 3:

S

M

A

R

T

NOTES:

Transform • Rachel Eva

WEEK 5

ACKNOWLEDGE GROWTH & NEXT STEP CHALLENGES

Be in the now. Be present.

Stop right here and congratulate yourself on your commitment to growing in wellness, wholeness and balance in order to become the best version of yourself and live the best life possible! Seriously, pat yourself on the back a bit because you deserve it! Popular culture provides so many mind-numbing distractions that keep you from investing time in your true growth and wellness.

Getting to week four is *no small victory*, it's a HUGE one!!!! So take a minute to reflect on the last month and all of the progress that you have made. Yes, now...right now...stop and intentionally think some positive thoughts about yourself and the victories and growth you have had in this program.

It's a journey and the destination should be kept in mind, aimed for intentionally and yet, the joy should be in the journey. Our minds, our bodies, our hearts (emotions) and our spirit continually need to be cared for, intentionally developed and assessed. This also means that as you move through your journey with clear goals and effective actions you will need to re-evaluate and adjust. Give yourself permission to change or expand your goals. What is right in this season for you may not be in the next one. As you learn more about yourself you may need to give yourself permission to change your goals and strategies to achieving them.

Just like a heart attack usually starts off as a heart condition before it escalates to a state of crisis, an injury or problem begins with a weakness or imbalance. This imbalance might be in any or all of the four systems; mental, emotional, physical or spiritual that leads to problems or undesired results. Many times this is aided by the choices you make or your perception of the circumstances you encounter. So whether you have a full-fledged problem a weakness or imbalance, it is important to connect with yourself and uncover it now so that you can take effective actions.

Where do you need to course correct? What areas are 'at risk' or needing more attention, time and resources? Meditate on that for a moment. What does your gut say? You may not 'feel' anything or any response. In this culture people suppress and ignore the gut feeling or intuition so much that it gets harder and harder to connect or differentiate from the internal thoughts resulting from fears and limiting beliefs.

Get back in touch with your intuition and build your mental, emotional, physical and spiritual connection. This will help you to make choices that are aligned or congruent with your true self.

EXERCISES

Continue your meditation practice and journal *daily*!

BUILDING RAPPORT WITH YOURSELF

Sit quietly, close your eyes and say the following: "I would like my intuition or gut to speak louder to me. I would like to develop my ability to HEAR, trust and listen to it."

Continue to sit and meditate on this thought for a few minutes while setting this as an intention: To hear, trust and listen to my gut/intuition.

LISTENING TO YOUR GUT

Practice listening to your 'gut'; your intuition and how it arises in any of your systems. Take notice of that inner voice or inner prompting. It may be small and quiet at first. It may come in the form of silly things like the thought of "don't forget to grab a sweater" when leaving the house. In those moments *follow* this prompt and *trust it even if it doesn't make sense (as long as its safe and ecological to do so)*. For example, the intuitive message of 'grab a sweater!'... It might be 90 degrees in the shade at 4 p.m. when you leave, but if you get stuck outdoors at midnight with a flat tire on your car—having a sweater makes sense, so trust and go with it, your intuitive intelligence may know best. We tend to want to understand and mentally (from a thought based place) make sense of intuitive gut messages before we validate and act on them. However to truly begin to deepen the connection and trust with your intuition we need to put common intellect to the side. The mind provides a different form of intelligence then our gut. Many times the problem comes when you try to translate a gut message into an organized thought that makes sense intellectually. Begin experimenting with following your gut. As long as you feel an intuitive or gut message is leading you towards something that is not harmful towards you, community and the world it is most likely safe to act upon. It will take time to develop the skill of differentiating random thoughts from a true intuitive gut message so be patient and consistent with practicing this!

As you discover and experience this write about these promptings and your progress. An example of how to journal about this:

As I was doing _____ I experienced, noticed or felt a

gut/intuition leading me to do _____ and my response was to

_____

_____

_____

and….

…I spent 30 minutes sitting silently, following my breath. As thoughts came into my mind, I did not get into a relationship with or judge them. I lovingly acknowledged them and let them go. I sat and actively LISTENED to my intuition or gut. In doing this I experienced, learned and felt:

UPDATE YOUR ACTION PLAN

Review some of your discoveries and journal entries. Also think about which actions you have been taking that seem to be leading towards balance, wellness and wholeness.
Ask yourself:

1. "Which actions have been effective so far?"
2. "Do I need to add, change or adjust any of my action plan steps?"

BELOW MAKE A LIST OF ADDITIONS OR CHANGES TO YOUR ACTION PLAN:

Mental system action steps:

1.

2.

3.

4.

5.

Emotional system action steps:

1.

2.

3.

4.

5.

Physical system action steps:

1.

2.

3.

4.

5.

Spiritual system action steps:

1.

2.

3.

4.

5.

NOTES:

Transform • Rachel Eva

Transform • Rachel Eva

Transform • Rachel Eva

Transform • Rachel Eva

WEEK 6

PUTTING THINGS IN RIGHT ORDER

At the end of the day, most people want to have their needs met, experience happiness, health, success and love (of course everyone has their own unique definitions of what those are). So your list of daily wants and needs must balance with your list of priorities and the conflicts that arise between them. Remember that what you think is your problem may not always be your problem and what you think is your solution may not always be your solution.

ASSESSING NEEDS VS. WANTS, DISCOVERING PRIORITIES, UNCOVERING CONFLICTS

When people begin this program in integrative wellness and wholeness, they usually have some issue that is a very high priority for them to work on. It's what they consider to be the problem or the issue they most want help to resolve. It's important to address that specifically through very clear and effective action steps, and at the same time, it's also important to identify needs versus wants in order to determine additional priorities that need to be addressed and to prevent any additional problems from being created.

How you determine your priorities is through taking the information discovered through your Self Discovery Form, as well as the Action Graph that you created (the graph that shows what the problem/issue is, why it's a problem, what steps you have already taken to try to resolve it and new action steps you can take to move towards your goal). You will also take all of the information you have collected and discovered about yourself over the course of the program, look at all of the things that are out of balance and you will see how many of them fall within a certain system. For example, there might be five different things that are out of balance in your physical system but only two things out of balance in your emotional system. Having that many things out of balance makes your physical system a priority, a need versus a want because the need to address that system first is urgent. Imbalances in your physical system could be leading you towards illness or injury. Another example could be: Discovering that one problem or issue has such a huge impact on all other areas of life and all of the four systems that it becomes the highest priority to address.

So, again, taking a look from a bigger picture perspective of that Action Graph that you created, to see where the most things are out of balance, then taking that information, compare that to your goals. Journal on what you uncover!

WELLNESS JOURNAL

Continue your daily journaling and add the progress you have been making in your action plan.

ACTION GRAPH COMPARISON

Take your original action graph (found in week three) on each area; mental, emotional, physical and spiritual and using these, create another Action Graph for each major area of life; relationships, family, health, career and finances, self-development and your spiritual life.

Next, compare the old Action Graph to your new Action Graph and also to your list of values and your SMART goals to discover conflicts. All of your action steps should be good for self, family, community and the world. Meaning all actions should be ecological. If one of your action steps or goals would cause harm to your family while bettering your finances and career, that would not be ecological. All actions, in order to be balanced and sustainable need to be ecological.

Another place to discover conflicts within your values is to look at what goals and actions are not in alignment with your values or with each other. For example, when you have a personal goal of 'more family time' and a work value of 'travel in order to create success' the two goals are in conflict or at the very least are working against each other! You must find a way to create congruency. Find a way the two goals can co-exist together at the same time while also being good for self, good for family, good for community and good for world. How one might do this is by redefining their views on 'family time' and 'travel'...possibly this could mean combining the two. Get ecologically creative, remember you are the co-creator of your life.

MAPPING CONFLICTS

Here is an exercise in mapping your values and discovering potential conflicts in your life. Once you get a clear picture, you can make decisions based on the best outcome for yourself and those who are part of your life.

HERE IS AN EXAMPLE OF THE MAPPING EXERCISE:

Action	Value (and SMART Goal)	Items In Conflict with Action
Working in a cubicle from 9-5	Freedom of schedule/create a job working flexible hours in nature making $xx by xx date.	My job is opposite of my value

EXERCISE:

Action	Value (and SMART Goal)	Items In Conflict with Action

Once you have completed this exercise, journal on ways to bring conflicting items into alignment.

Transform • Rachel Eva

NOTES:

Transform • Rachel Eva

Transform • Rachel Eva

Transform • Rachel Eva

WEEK 7

SELF CARE

By taking care of yourself, you are investing in time well spent for you—and the other people in your life. One of the most powerful boundaries you set is a boundary with yourself regarding your care and treatment of yourself and the time, energy and resources that you invest in doing so.

Think of yourself as a bank account. You can't give out what you do not have yourself. This means that making 'deposits' of time, thought, rest and other ways of appreciating yourself allow you to have more love, care, concern, energy and assistance to share or give away. If your life requires the care of others such as family members, friendships and co-workers think of the deposits you make in yourself as the fuel that will empower you with the energy to take care of all of the other responsibilities your life holds.

So give yourself permission to love yourself. Give yourself permission to take care of yourself first and foremost as a priority!

THE "ME TIME" EXERCISE

The "Me Time" exercise is a time once a week where you schedule one to three hours to do something by yourself, with yourself and for yourself. This activity can be anything from taking a walk in the park to getting a facial or massage. In order to bring balance into your life, as well as to better your relationship with yourself, this exercise is an important ongoing practice—so keep it on your list, and keep it a priority. This should be done each week, ongoing as part of your normal schedule.

If you want to have a good relationship with someone, you need to invest time and attention in the relationship. The same is true with your own self. How can you have a good relationship with yourself without making any investment in you? So, the "Me Time" exercise creates an opportunity for investment for you to build, grow and strengthen your relationship with your self. Before you start this exercise, give some thought to your self-image. How in love with you are you? If you are feeling anything less than love, make an appointment with yourself right now and make an intention that you will find truth, beauty and goodness in all parts of yourself.

"Me Time" date, time, place, items to bring, cost and any other details:

Transform • Rachel Eva

DATE NIGHT WITH SELF

The "Date Night with Self" exercise is meant for building self-value, worth and self-perception. Whether you are a man or a woman, this exercise is for you to do with and for yourself. It may be an odd concept for you to grasp, however, the feedback I've got from clients that have done this exercise has been so positive!

Make a date for yourself (this can be an hour or a whole day, it can be done in the day time or the night time, it can cost money or be completely free)—take yourself out to do some activity on your own. Plan it with events and activities that you'd want to experience on the best date of your life. For example, going out to dinner and a movie, or going to happy hour then to the theater. One client took herself on a hot air balloon ride for her date!

"Date Night with Self" plan:

_____

_____

_____

_____

_____

_____

After you have completed the "Me Time" and "Date Night with Self" exercises, write about them your wellness journal.

Transform • Rachel Eva

Transform • Rachel Eva

NOTES:

Transform • Rachel Eva

Transform • Rachel Eva

WEEK 8

GRATITUDE & HAPPINESS

Happiness is a choice. In times of resistance, when I've been rebelling against letting go of habits or resentments that I feel justified in having, I've been reminded that it is impossible to be miserable when you're grateful. In those moments the very last thing I feel is grateful. Writing a "gratitude list" seems silly and is the last thing I feel like doing, no matter how perky and happy the person is who recommends that I re-focus on gratitude.

Yet, I have found that it is in fact absolutely, completely and totally impossible to be sad, angry, bitter, resentful, and lonely if I'm feeling honest gratitude!

I know this because I've experimented with it many times. Each time I chose to put negative feelings on the shelf and turn my focus to all the things that I am grateful for I always find that positive feelings soon follow. Why? When a person magnifies something, it gets bigger.

When you chose to magnify feelings of gratitude, they become so big and beautiful that it literally shrinks the negative feelings and makes you better able to cope with issues. What do you have to be grateful for? Start with your ability to change the things that don't make you happy or the simple fact that you are alive today and able to consider change!

Happiness is a choice. Joy is a choice, too, and it's available for you to make right now in this moment.

GRATITUDE EXERCISE

There is a huge difference between affirmational and authentic gratitude. Affirmational gratitude is telling yourself a lie. Example: "I am grateful because I have everything that I need," when in reality that person believes they are lacking what they need—and may be doing a "fake it 'til you make it" kind of action. That kind of gratitude is false, and not effective. It is essentially just a lie you are telling yourself.

Authentic gratitude is discovering something, even the small, simple things, to be grateful for, feeling the truth of it in your heart, and writing it on a gratitude list. If you are having a hard time feeling grateful for things, or don't have anything to be grateful for, flip forward to the "Finding the Beauty" exercises and do them before moving back to the Gratitude exercise.

The "Gratitude" exercise is very simple. Simply write a gratitude list. Bring things to mind by asking yourself what you're grateful for within each of the major areas of your life: health, relationships, family, career and finances, self-development and spirituality.

WHAT AM I GRATEFUL FOR?

My gratitude list:

1.

2.

3.

4.

5.

6.

7.

8.

9.

10.

FINDING THE BEAUTY EXERCISES

Our brains develop unconscious patterns. Many times these are completely unintentional patterns that have a negative effect on our lives when played out over time. We literally train our brains, like a puppy to fetch certain information. For example; fetch that shoe in puppy training could be; fetch that negative piece of information in our brain training. When this happens over and over it becomes an unconscious pattern. This is one of the ways people develop unconscious beliefs and patterns. Our brains are systematic and sweep through our every day life collecting and storing only tiny bits of information in our conscious minds. The good news is that we can intentionally reprogram, rewire and retrain our brains to notice, collect and store information that will support our highest good and happiness. It does take repetition, just like training a puppy, and consistency.

Read this brain re-training exercise below and then make it a point to begin practicing it daily. Write it all down so that you can track your progress and your discoveries.

FINDING THE BEAUTY IN OTHERS

Today I noticed (anything positive) _____

about _____ and...

I thought _____ and

I shared with _____ the following words

FINDING THE BEAUTY IN SELF

Today I noticed _____ about myself and

I thought _____ and

I shared with _____ the following words

_____

_____

FINDING THE BEAUTY IN THE WORLD

Today I noticed _____ about

_____ and

I thought _____ and

I shared with _____ the following words

_____

_____

FINDING THE BEAUTY IN THE CHALLENGE

Today I noticed _____ about (the challenge I'm facing) and …

I thought _____ and

I shared with _____ the following words

_____

_____

FINDING THE BEAUTY IN THE LESSON/LEARNING

From these things today I discovered _____ (the learning or lesson) and this lesson/learning will help make my life more beautiful in the following ways:

1.

2.

3.

NOTES:

Transform • Rachel Eva

Transform • Rachel Eva

WEEK 9

CREATING BALANCE

What is balance, anyway? Balance looks different for every person, every lifestyle and every set of goals within any season of a persons life. Finding balance is a journey of self-discovery and an artful practice of self-love and self-care. And, on this journey, there is no end-place or destination; there are only stops along the way. If you pay attention, you'll notice that everything just keeps getting better—the more you do and the more you learn.

Imagine a person walking on a tightrope. Moment to moment they have to shift their weight and make adjustments in order to stay centered on the tightrope so they will not fall. This is a perfect image for understanding balance in all areas of your life. It takes moment-to-moment adjustments, intentionality and focus.

The questions for a deep dive into the concept of balance are these:

1. Are you approaching the learning how to take care of yourself with love in a balanced way?
2. Have you stopped a need to fix yourself in order to be accepted, desired, loved, approved or good enough?
3. Are you consistently caring for and treating yourself with love?

Wellness and balance go hand in hand. You cannot have one without the other. Find balance and you will find wellness and vice versa. Balance takes daily time, energy and intentionality! May you always choose to BE balanced today!

YOUR "WHY'S?" OR REASONS

In your journal write a list of the reasons why you want to achieve your goals. Be honest with yourself and ask yourself if they are rooted in loving self-care or judgment, a need for approval or based on the expectations of other people.

Here is an example of how to do this:

My "Why?" or my reason for:

...being healthy is _____

_____

_____

_____

_____

...being in my career is _____

_____

_____

_____

_____

...being successful is

...being in a relationship with _____ is

Add any others that come to mind...

My "Why?" or my reason for:

...being _____ is

Transform • Rachel Eva

...being _____ is _____

...being _____ is _____

...being _____ is _____

GETTING MORE INTENTIONAL WITH BALANCE

Now that you've generated a lot of material with respect to your life and patterns, go back through all you've written and re-read it in Week Nine. Make any changes, adjustments or additions that you now see are necessary to move towards having more self love and balance.

CREATE A DAILY SELF-CARE TO DO LIST

Now that you've learned to practice self-care with the "Me Time" exercise and by taking yourself out for a fun date, pay attention to what you do for yourself over the course of a day. Make a list of things that take care of self, reinforce good habits and bring more balance to your self-care.

Your list should include self-care in all four systems; mental, emotional, physical and spiritual. Here's an example:

1. Meditate
2. Read
3. Exercise for one hour
4. Eat healthy and drink plenty of water
5. Spend quality time in fun activities with loved ones
6. Do the actions from my Action Plan to move me from where I am now to where I want to be
7. Be 100 percent present and focused at work
8. Do my best

Create your daily self care list:

1. _____
_____
_____
_____

2.

3.

4.

5.

6.

7.

8.

9.

10.

NOTES:

Transform • Rachel Eva

Transform • Rachel Eva

WEEK 10

PURPOSE

Discovering your purpose can seem like a very BIG concept, but there is a way to simplify it. You have a purpose behind every choice you make and behind every action you take. Some are conscious and some are unconscious. The higher purpose or reason you make one choice or take one action over another can be as simple as "to be happy," "to be safe" or "to be loved." Discovering your purpose starts with the bigger picture, the main idea behind what drives you.

Some people know what their career purpose is, or their place in the family and yet have no understanding of the greater purpose behind their roles. I think it is important to know both. The questions you ask in the area of purpose and 'driving forces' lead you deeper into self-discovery, fulfillment and a deeper meaning and enjoyment of life. Understanding and living your purpose *on* purpose, or with *intention and attention*, is a lifelong adventure!

All of the discovery tools within this section include two elements:

1. Asking questions
2. Journaling

Answer the questions honestly and without fear. Now and then expand on them as you dive deeper in your journal. Write with freedom and total abandon! There is no need to edit or filter your thoughts; just let them flow freely and without judgment.

QUESTIONS TO ASK

Imagine that you were free to create and experience anything you wanted to in your life. What if there were no barriers? Dream big! What would you want in your life, what would you want to experience or create? With this in mind fill in the rest of the sentences below:

I want to be

I want to experience

I want to do

I want to create _____

_____

_____

_____.

I am passionate about _____

_____

_____

_____.

POINTS TO PONDER

We have patterns for a reason. Most of the negative patterns are strategies to achieving something positive, they just have ceased to be effective and helpful strategies. Let's discover what the reasons are behind some negative patterns or limiting beliefs and behaviors you identified that you have. After you do, fill in the rest of the sentence:

Why I do _____ is, or I do _____

because _____

_____

_____

_____

_____.

Now let's try to see what the bigger, higher purpose behind that action, pattern, strategy or behavior is by answering the following question:

What is the higher purpose of doing that?

NOTES:

Transform • Rachel Eva

Transform • Rachel Eva

Transform • Rachel Eva

Transform • Rachel Eva

WEEK 11

STEPPING INTO EMPOWERMENT, WELLNESS & WHOLENESS

I Am.

You are.

The entire concept of "I am" is one that you have the power to define and to create. Throughout the preceding weeks you did a lot of self-discovery and brought more wholeness into your life.

PONDER THESE QUESTIONS AND WRITE YOUR ANSWERS:

1. What has this experience taught you?

Transform • Rachel Eva

2. What have taking these steps empowered you to see, do or create differently?

Empowerment is when you recognize your ability to create your own life and when you become willing to let go of what doesn't serve you and to take the actions necessary to create new outcomes. You are in charge of your mind, your beliefs and your perceptions. You are empowered to create the life you want. Being empowered doesn't mean you control others or the world around you. It means you take responsibility and effective actions to create yourself and therefore your view of and way in which you experience the world.

JOURNAL EXERCISE

Journal the concept of "I am." Your "I am" is how you would define your truest self (not someone else's definition or expectation of who you are). Also write about how you are empowered—how you give yourself permission to be you. Get specific and pour it all out onto the lines below or in your journal.

Transform • Rachel Eva

NOTES:

Transform • Rachel Eva

Transform • Rachel Eva

Transform • Rachel Eva

WEEK 12

CELEBRATE!

The joy is in the journey and it's also about *celebrating* the journey! It is easy to lose focus and get stuck in the habit of looking at your life, your self and your goals with blinders on—where you only see an "end goal" or desired "outcome." Life is about living. It is about the things you learn and the learnings you collect from each and every experience you encounter. Truly living is when you are hunting for your learnings, being intentional about continuing self-development, growing and moving towards wholeness.

It is in the moment that you are whole.

No one tells you this! The moment that you realize that "the moment" is all you have—when you feel that concept as your truth—you become free to be yourself and to know yourself as a beautiful creature who is always a *work in progress*. Knowing this gives you emotional freedom—and within that freedom is the ability to know greater love, confidence and compassion for others. It allows you to harmonize with your external reality in a new way.

So, celebrate the amazing leanings and experiences you have collected from this adventure of the *Transform* program. Choose a way to celebrate it as well as your commitment to this program. Maybe you'll take yourself on a special date, or add some new form of self-care or throw a dance party for yourself in your living room. Perhaps you'll create new words of affirmation, or do something with unconditional love—without any expectation of a return—for someone else. You now know so much more about yourself: how you are wired; what is important to you and why; the best habits for you; the best practices for nutrition and communicating with others—and perhaps even more happened to you than either you or I could have predicted. You have made huge steps on your own personal journey simply by reading this, so I congratulate you and I celebrate you!

FIND A WAY TO CELEBRATE!

Write in your journal what you have learned at this point in the process of this program.

Share your experience with another person (partner, friend, neighbor, doctor, therapist, co-worker or family member). When you grow and become empowered it is important to share your experience with others. Sharing your story may be the exact inspiration someone else needs at that moment.

Your experience is a gift. Pay it forward.

BRING IT ALL HOME

Now let's bring everything together in one last exercise to clarify and document what you learned, what you got out of this program and also what specific growth or changes you have seen take place over the 12 weeks.

Journal on your take-aways as defined above:

NEXT STEPS

It is important to continue your journey to *Transform*. I recommend that you continue to take the steps you identified as effective actions. I also recommend you continue to evaluate your beliefs, let go of the ones that don't serve you and dive deeper into self-development.

Again, this is a life long journey, not an event. Think of your self-development as an 'infinite onion' with many layers to peel. Once you peel through one, continue on to the next one! Watch as this 'infinite onion' grows new layers for you to discover! This journey is what makes life such a wonderful, rich and beautiful experience. Remember that you can reinvent your life and reinvent yourself any time you want to. Give yourself permission to do so because you are empowered!

Your last step within this 12-week program is to write out an Action Plan for moving forward. Using all of the tools, techniques and exercises within this curriculum, please write out a new plan! Find someone with whom you can share your plan with and who can and will hold you accountable. After writing a 'next steps' plan of action out, share it with your accountability partner or a friend in order to gain support, resources and to track your movement forward.

Be intentional about all of your next steps, about getting and implementing resources, and staying accountable and connected. Wellness is a verb, an action word, and for a wellness plan to work it must be filled with *intentional* actions.

May you be, achieve and experience all that leads you towards wholeness and your true self!

In Wholeness,

Rachel Eva

NEXT STEP ACTION PLAN:

Transform • Rachel Eva

Transform • Rachel Eva

MY THREE INVITATIONS TO YOU...

1. If you felt that my teaching style and information was helpful, I invite you to check out my online courses, seminars, other books, blogs and workshops by visiting RachelEvaOnline.com as well as by keeping connected through social media (@RachelEvaOnline), Twitter - Facebook - Instagram I would love to hear how this information unfolds in your life and assists you on your path!

2. My second ask is that if you got something out of this book and feel it is valuable, share it with the world and those you love! Here are a few ways to do that:

1. Write a review on Amazon
2. Share it on Facebook
3. Share it on Twitter
4. Take a photo of you with the book and post it on Instagram (if you do this, tag me! I love seeing your faces!)

3. Live full on! Keep going and keep growing more and more into the full wholeness of your authentic and best self.

RECOMMENDED READING FOR CONTINUED GROWTH

The Textbook for Integrative Wellness and Life Coaching, Rachel Eva

Playing Full Out, Rachel Eva

The Holographic Universe, Michael Talbott

Loving What Is, Byron Katie

You Can Heal Your Life, Louise Hay

Quantum Healing, Deepak Chopra

Healing Back Pain, John E. Sarno

The Biology of Belief, Bruce Lipton

Skinny Bitch, Rory Freedman

The Makers Diet, Jordan Rubin

The Paleo Solution, Robb Wolf

The Paleo Diet: Lose Weight and Get Healthy by Eating the Foods You Were Designed to Eat, Loren Cordain

The Five Levels of Attachment, Don Miguel Ruiz, Jr.

The Four Agreements, Don Miguel Ruiz

The Five Love Languages, Gary D. Chapman

The Honeymoon Effect, Bruce Lipton

Clean, Alejandro Junger, M.D.

Integrate The Shadow, Master Your Path, Dr. Matthew B James (DrMatt.com)

Mental Emotional Release®, Dr. Matthew B. James (DrMatt.com)

Mitakuye Oyasin: We Are All Related, A. C. Ross

The Yoga Sutras of Patanjali, Swami Satchidananda

Love & Respect, Emmerson Eggerichs

Boundaries: When to Say Yes, How to Say No to Take Control of Your Life, Henry Cloud & John Townsend

The Grief Recovery Handbook, John W. James and Russell Friedman

Blink: The Power of Thinking without Thinking, Malcolm Gladwell

Live Your Truth, Kamal Ravikant

Love Yourself Like Your Life Depends On It, Kamal Ravikant

Start with Why, Simon Sinek (and I also recommend his TedTalk)

The Healing Code, Alexander Loyd

Bruce Lee Fighting Spirit, Bruce Thomas

The Makers Diet, Jordan Rubin

One Big Thing, Phil Cook

Seven Habits of Highly Successful People, Steven Covey

The Foundation of Huna, Matthew B. James

You're Not Sick, You're Thirsty, F. Batmanghelidj

The China Study: The Most Comprehensive Study of Nutrition Ever Conducted and the Startling Implications for Diet, Weight Loss, and Long-term Health, Thomas Campbell

Frequency, Penny Peirce

Human Tuning, John Beaulieu

RESOURCES

RECOMMENDED MOVIES AND VIDEOS

"What the Bleep Do We Know!?"
"I am"
"The Matrix" (for visual understanding of quantum theory)
"The Secret"
"The 13th Floor" (for visual understanding of quantum theory)
"The Shift" (with Dr. Wayne Dyer)
"Forks over Knives" (documentary about food)
"DeMartini: Personifying the Quantum Theory"
"Joseph Campbell and The Power of Myth with Bill Moyers"

TEDTALKS

1. Nadine Burke Harris: "How Childhood Trauma Affects Health Across a Lifetime"
2. Jill Bolte Taylor: "My Stroke of Insight"
3. Sam Richards: "A Radical Experiment in Empathy"
4. Zak Ebrahim: I am the Son of a Terrorist. Here's How I Chose Peace."
TED's playlist on forgiveness: TED.com/playlists/213/how_and_why_to_forgive

ONLINE COURSES AND BLOGS TO FOLLOW

RachelEvaOnline.com
IntegrativeWellnessAcademy.com

NOTES

Transform • Rachel Eva

Transform • Rachel Eva